LEADERSHIP
MADE SIMPLE

PRACTICAL SOLUTIONS TO YOUR
GREATEST MANAGEMENT CHALLENGES

LEADERSHIP MADE SIMPLE

ED OAKLEY
DOUG KRUG

ENLIGHTENED
LEADERSHIP
SOLUTIONS

PUBLICATIONS

Enlightened Leadership Publications
5380 South Monaco Street, Suite 700
Greenwood Village, CO 80111
303-729-0540
www.enleadership.com
www.leadershipmadesimple.com

First Edition, 2006
Manufactured in Canada
10 9 8 7 6 5 4 3 2
Library of Congress Control Number: 2006928164
Publisher's Cataloging-in-Publication Data
Oakley, Ed
Leadership made simple: practical solutions to your greatest management challenges
Includes index.
1.   Leadership. 2. Management. 3. Organizational Effectiveness
I.   Krug, Doug. II. Title.
ISBN 10: 1-890088-19-6
ISBN 13: 978-1-890088-19-4

Edited by Peter Gerardo and Helenita Ziegler
Illustrations by Lindsey Bergman
Book Design by Desktop Publishing Ltd.

Advanced Praise for *Leadership Made Simple*

"The 'five magic questions' of the Framework for Leadership are so flexible and creative that they can be used at every level of an organization with astonishing success. They are incredible for implementing change management. I highly recommend this book."

H. Joseph Marshall, Ph.D.
Managing Partner
Resource Management of Boston

"Just finished the book! A great down-to-earth approach to leadership. Your examples and simple yet effective processes allowed me to immediately begin solving problems in my head as I read with the forward focus. Congratulations!"

Dr. Kevin D. Gazzara
Strategy & Design Program Manager
Intel Corporation

"In a world where our leaders are overwhelmed with all that needs doing...this book is a breath of fresh air! The authors deliver on their promise. They provide their audience with a straightforward way of guiding others. Even the busiest of leaders can make time for this."

Beverly Kaye
CEO/Founder, Career Systems International
Co-Author, Love 'Em or Lose 'Em:
Getting Good People to Stay

"*Leadership Made Simple* is excellent! This will be a book read well and often by decision-makers and their teams. I like the examples throughout. It's a winner!"

Nido Qubein
President, High Point University
Chairman, Great Harvest Bread Company

"Leadership generally defies description, however the book reminds us that it need not be mystical, or something that one is born to alone. It can be learned, and *Leadership Made Simple* is just that, a simple guide to how to learn."

Stuart Ochiltree
Chairman, Univera LifeSciences

"*Leadership Made Simple* sends a good message! I am a firm believer that a good 'manager' is not always a good 'leader.' The Framework for Leadership will certainly help us in the development of future leaders. It has already worked for me!"

Dave Malenfant
Vice President, Global Supply Chain
Alcon Laboratories

"This book demystifies what it takes to be a true leader but also does it in a simplified way that enables the reader to put the principles into effect immediately and start leading with positive results that provide long-term solutions. Very well done."

Ken Banks
CEO, KAB Marketing

"I am inspired by your book! I realize the importance of investing critical time with project teams *before* starting on the action plan. I can clearly see how your simple, yet vital process will increase the quality of, and buy-in for, the plan."

Ralph Johnson
Project Manager
IBM Global Services

"Effective communications is vital within and between organizations and their stakeholders. This excellent book provides a powerful framework for making that happen smoothly — even when conflict is involved."

Jeff Julin, President
MGA Communications

"THE key tool that every small business owner needs to help him/her bridge the gap between just managing and really leading. Read it today."

Carol Bergmann, Author,
Managing Your Energy at Work:
The Key to Unlocking Hidden Potential
in the Workplace

"Einstein said the hardest part of discovering the Theory of Relativity was 'determining how to think about it.' He was seeking a framework from which to explore the information that could lead him to his goal. *Leadership Made Simple* is such a tool. It provides the framework that takes the confusion out of things. Life is actually pretty simple, but living it successfully is a challenge. Leadership is pretty simple too, if you have the right guides and the discipline to follow them. Now you do."

Jim Cathcart, author, Relationship Selling,
founder, 101 Leaders Alliance.
www.cathcart.com

Acknowledgments

Acknowledging people who helped develop *Leadership Made Simple* is one of the most rewarding aspects of the book project, as well as the most challenging. It is rewarding because the book is finished, and we get to reflect with gratitude about the people who were such an important part of this project. It is challenging because so many people helped in many different ways, and we are afraid we might leave out someone in our expression of gratitude.

We give credit for much of the quality of the writing to its primary editors, Peter Gerardo and Helenita Ziegler. We consider ourselves more authors than good writers. You both are much appreciated, and you should be proud of the results.

We thank Daniel Yaeger for his cover design, and Jim Bisakowski for the interior design and layout. We appreciate Lindsey Bergman for providing the internal graphics and Cheryl Bonnell for skillfully managing many administrative details. Reya Ingle proved to be a valuable and proficient final editor.

Ginny Hill's eagle eye caught a number of last-minute typos in a final read that saved us embarrassment. Thank you, friend.

We consider "peer reviews" one of the most important aspects of writing a non-fiction book. We were so blessed in having a number of proven leaders generously offer their time, energy and talent to review the manuscript and give us feedback about what they liked and ways it could be even better. Those "even betters" took the book to a much higher level of effectiveness, quality, under-standability, usefulness, and value while the "what they liked" kept us inspired to keep moving forward on the project. These people included our friends and colleagues Carol Bergmann, Larry Cooper, Jonette Crowley, Jackie Fouse, Alan Gay, George Metanias, Ned Minor and Colleen Stanley. We are so grateful for your encouragement and honest feedback that made this a much better book.

Two people who were especially encouraging were A.J. Hiltenbrand and Lee Casaleggio. We appreciate you!

Then there are the real heroes of the book. They are the clients, colleagues and family members who provided the leadership that created the stories and case studies to tell. They stepped up their leadership, used the concepts and tools and created the successes that we get to share.

We are especially grateful to our families, who continue to be such a source of encouragement and inspiration for all we do. And a warm thank you to Ed's mastermind group for applying the appropriate peer pressure and encouragement over several years to get this project done. They include Ken Banks, Marjorie Brody, Terri Kabachnick, Brian Lee, Bob Romano and Barbara Sanfilippo.

Lastly, we thank you, the reader, in advance for the ways you will make a difference by applying the essence of *Leadership Made Simple*. We hope to hear from you about your successes as you continue to raise your level of leadership higher and higher.

With much gratitude,

Ed & Doug

To all of you striving to make a difference by providing the best leadership you can. We are blessed to be able to serve you.

Contents

Introduction

Simplicity is the ultimate sophistication.
Leonardo da Vinci

The goal of *Leadership Made Simple* is to simplify many of your complex leadership challenges into a useable, understandable and actionable framework. For nearly two decades our firm has had the privilege of working with many leaders and their teams from all levels in organizations large and small. We have been teaching and utilizing our Framework for Leadership™ as a simple tool for dealing with complex leadership/management challenges. Regardless of the circumstances, from complex process solutions to development programs to specific workshops, we have trusted the simple process even when we could not predict how it would lead to the outcomes that were sought. Yet, repeatedly, the process did work – with the solutions revealing themselves, sometimes spontaneously and sometimes gradually. Often the solutions were incremental improvements, and many times they were transformational.

The Framework has worked to:

- turn around large, failing projects.
- resolve conflicts between people and teams.
- establish shared visions.
- create buy-in for a project among many stakeholders.
- solve problems both simple and complex.
- determine breakthrough growth strategies.
- even reconnect quarreling family members.

The Framework for Leadership naturally shifts participants from a problem orientation to a solutions orientation, a simple but profound shift, and it often works even more effectively when the situation seems the most challenging. A communicative, collaborative environment is created that invites solutions to evolve from the people closest to the issue. "The basis of leadership is the capacity of the leader to change the mindset, the framework of the other person,"[1] said Warren Bennis, noted leadership authority and author of numerous books on the subject.

You can take a class on conflict resolution, another on problem-solving, still another on managing projects, decision-making, etc. Or, you can experiment with the essence of this Framework – this simple tool – and begin to see clearly how the answers to your greatest challenges are already available if you just trust the process. The essence of this Framework is a part of our firm's soul, and it has been invaluable in its ability to help us and our clients see things in a new, more effective, light.

While it would be easy to begin with the entire Framework for Leadership, it is important to develop the background for this process, as well as each of the steps that are involved. Since every step has its own purpose and value, each could be used separately as well as part of the larger process.

While the Framework is simple, it is not simplistic.

The Simple Truth about Leadership

"I knew then and believe even more firmly now – there is a simpler way to lead organizations, one that requires less effort and produces less stress than the current practices."[2]

Meg Wheatley, Ph.D.
Leadership and the New Science

We have been deceived into thinking that leadership is some complex, mysterious ability that only a few special people possess. But, in fact, leadership is something that virtually everyone does provide at certain times. We would also argue that leadership *must* be simple in order to succeed.

Management vs. Leadership

Every organizational process has its "hard" part and "soft" part. The hard part includes structures, systems, procedures, processes, rules, tools, controls, plans, etc. The soft part involves people – their creativity, attitudes, energy, focus, emotions, buy-in, resistance to change, fears and level of trust, or lack thereof.

To be a completely effective manager, you must manage *things* and lead your *people* – and the latter is usually more challenging.

Management concentrates on the hard components, while leadership focuses on the soft ones. To be a completely effective manager, you must manage *things* and lead your *people* – and the latter is usually more challenging.

We surveyed managers from more than 65 countries and hundreds of companies with the same question: "Which is more difficult – the hard part or the soft part?" Regardless of culture or country, the answer was almost always the same: "The soft part."

Surprised?

We didn't think so.

If you're like many managers, your training was focused almost exclusively on the hard parts. And, if you received an education in a highly technical competency such as engineering, physics, accounting, information technology or medicine, your attention was probably drawn even further from the soft side. No wonder so many struggle with leadership!

This is not to say that management should take a back seat to leadership, or that the soft aspect is more important than the hard. On the contrary, each is a critical part of effective management. What's important is striking a balance between the two on a continual basis. Focusing on one part and ignoring the other is not likely to work for long. This was learned the hard way at our own performance consulting company when we relied too heavily on the soft/leadership part.

Our systems and processes were not keeping pace with our rapid growth, and until we directed sufficient attention and energy toward solving the hard issues, our company suffered. That internal experience led us to focus our work with clients on the balance of hard and soft to create measurable, sustainable results, which distinguishes us in the consulting business.

However, when you need to cope with change, or when your organization is in transition, or when you need to discover new directions so your company can thrive (or just survive), management alone is not enough. There are too many people issues. This is when leadership is really needed to provide inspiration and motivation to bring out the best in your people.

How do you lead effectively?

One thing is clear – it must be simple or it's not likely to work.

The Power of Simplicity

In his excellent book *The Power of Simplicity*, best-selling author Jack Trout said, "…business is not that complex. It's just that there are too many people out there making it complex. The way to fight complexity is to use simplicity."[3]

That's our view of leadership.

We had an example of the importance of simplicity while working in an oilfield production unit in Sumatra, Indonesia, where English was the typical manager's *third* language. We facilitated all the sessions in English without translation and quietly wondered if our clients really understood the Framework for Leadership process we were explaining or if they would be able to apply it in real-world situations. The power of simplicity was to be tested! Fortunately, they impressed us with the quality of their planning, problem-solving, creativity and solutions to real challenges. They did it all using our Framework for Leadership.

As a testimony to the success, John Baltz, then Vice President of the unit, left an urgent message that awaited our return to the United States. John had been a member of a small group that had used the Framework for Leadership in a real-life situation during the workshop, and the process was so valuable that he wanted to share the results with VP's of other divisions. He was calling to see where we had stored the easel charts for the exercise, so he could tell about the process and show its results to the other executives in his organization.

A complex process or tool would not have worked in that environment. A simple one did!

Although many aspects of leadership seem complex, they *can* be simplified, and most successful leaders recognize the importance of this. Indeed, the late An Wang, founder of Wang Labs, put this into perspective when he said, "No matter how complicated a problem is, it usually can be reduced to a simple, comprehensible form which is often the best solution."

That is the simple truth about leadership.

The Framework for Leadership™

Which of the following challenges do you face?

- Shifting resistance to change into wholehearted commitment.
- Solving problems with maximum creativity and minimum defensiveness.
- Aligning teams and stakeholders for optimum results.
- Gaining buy-in and ownership for what needs to be done.
- Resolving conflicts among people and cross-functional teams.
- Achieving breakthrough performance on even the most challenging projects.
- Motivating team members to be their best.
- Enhancing communication across departments.
- Developing a shared, inspiring vision and common objectives.
- Negotiating win-win agreements in challenging situations.
- Unleashing breakthrough creativity and innovation.
- Promoting cross-functional collaboration and teamwork.
- Making better decisions more quickly.
- Achieving better results from projects right from the start.
- Overcoming corporate inertia.
- Dealing with a difficult boss or subordinate.

Leadership Made Simple provides a specific, flexible and simple framework for dealing with these problems. In the following pages, we first provide the supportive background and concepts underlying the Framework. Then we present the practical, easy-to-use 5-step process that generates positive results – time after time. You will discover how to optimize results by balancing and integrating the systems/processes and the people/talent sides of your business.

Descriptive Overview of the Framework

1. Focus on the successes you are already having.
2. Analyze those successes for what made them work.
3. Continually clarify your goals or objectives.
4. Determine the benefits of achieving those objectives.
5. Establish an action plan and accountability.

Leadership Made Simple introduces a simple 5-step Framework for Leadership – a process that will help you produce immediate, tangible, real-world results. The Descriptive Overview above is not the actual Framework, but is just a hint of some key aspects of the Framework. In the next chapters, we will introduce some basic concepts and tools which will integrate into the full Framework for Leadership.

Where other approaches have failed to resolve difficult leadership challenges, the Framework for Leadership has consistently worked. The Framework has succeeded in turning around seemingly "doomed" projects, saving tens of millions of dollars, and in others generated millions of dollars in extra profits. It helped a federal agency achieve more progress in one year on a critical program than in the entire previous decade. It has also been used to transform dysfunctional family relationships into healthy ones.

You don't need an MBA to implement these ideas. And if you do have an MBA, *Leadership Made Simple* may just supply some of the missing pieces to your education.

Does this book contain everything you could ever want to know about leadership? No. But one of the best ways to develop leadership is to employ effective leadership tools and to learn from your experiences while using them. This book offers those proven tools.

Measurable Successes

Following are three examples of measurable successes that were achieved using the tools, concepts and attitudes that will be explained in *Leadership Made Simple:*

- A regional claim center of a major insurance company was in big trouble. With its customer service rating hovering at a miserable 58%, a senior manager was brought in to lead a turnaround. Using the concepts and tools found in this book, he took a very simple approach to the project – so simple that in the beginning it generated nay-saying and pushback from almost every quarter. Eighteen months later, his approach was vindicated: the claim center's customer service rating stood at 93% – making its program *the* benchmark for the rest of the company. The key to the effectiveness of his approach was its simplicity.

■ A.J. Hiltenbrand, former director of corporate executive development for a major pharmaceutical and surgical company, was determined to prove the bottom-line value of the soft-skills education his organization had provided for years. At the request of senior management, he implemented the "Finding Profit Workshop," using the tools in *Leadership Made Simple* in several foreign country markets. As a result of actions taken in direct response to the workshop; the Italian market reported a 10 to 1 return on investment (ROI); in Greece, the figure was 9 to 1; and in Turkey, 13 to 1. Bulgaria reported a staggering 48 to 1 ROI, which included an extra $984,000 in accounts receivable collected because of decisions made using the workshop process.

■ Penny Weismuller, manager of disease control for a major California county, used the tools in this book to support her team in developing collaborative, innovative solutions for housing communicable tuberculosis patients – a very expensive and previously "complex" problem. The simple, creative ideas they generated maintained the required isolation while saving $206,277 the first three months and $285,824 during the next three months. They anticipated similar quarterly savings going forward. Imagine the impact on the "bottom line."

We will address details of each of these examples in later chapters. We first need to provide some context and background for the leadership tools to be introduced, which we will do in the next chapter.

2

The Answers Are in the Room

"Leaders do not need to have all the answers.
They do need to ask the right questions."[4]
Ronald Heifitz and Donald Laurie
"The Work of Leadership,"
Harvard Business Review, February, 2000.

L eaders can no longer be expected to have all the answers. The world is far too complex for that. But when you access the creativity, knowledge, wisdom and spirit of your people – the answers are available within the organization. The experts are already there. The key is accessing those solutions.

Ed Oakley was waiting for a presentation on intellectual property rights along with 22 other professional speakers, consultants and trainers, when he noticed that the host kept ducking in and out of the room. Bob Wendover, a friend, author and speaker, did *not* look happy. Ed followed him out of the room, and asked if he could help. "The speaker is 30 minutes late," said Bob, "and I can't get in touch with him. It appears he's not going to show up! I think we're out of luck."

Ed proposed an idea and – with nothing to lose – Bob agreed to let him run the meeting.

"I believe the 'answers are in the room,'" Ed told the group. "I would like to test that belief." He asked the attendees to write down any questions they had about intellectual property rights. After the questions were collected, Ed read the first one, and asked, "Who has the answer to this question?" Three people raised their hands, and then addressed the question. Ed moved to the next question, and again asked who had the answer. Several people responded. This process continued for more than an hour until all but one question had been answered. The room was buzzing with energy.

The meeting was a phenomenal success, despite the absence of the expert – or perhaps *because* of his absence. If the attorney had shown up, he might have: (A) put half the audience to sleep; and (B) withheld specifics when asked detailed questions (details often require a significant consultation fee). After all, the attorney would have been there for his own marketing purposes.

To the benefit and surprise of the attendees, the answers were in the room. The same dynamic has proven itself over and over in the nearly two decades we have been introducing the concept to our clients.

Letting Go for the Best Solution

A good leader recognizes that she doesn't have – and doesn't need to have – the answer for every challenge encountered by the team. She releases her ego-driven desire to be the font of all knowledge, and instead launches a search for the best answer. She knows that leadership isn't about dispensing wisdom to wide-eyed supplicants. It *is* about harnessing team members' unique creativity, experiences and ideas to produce results that are greater than the sum of the individual abilities, and creating exceptional, even transformational results.

Author of the popular business novel, *The Goal,* Eli Goldratt said, "If you want people to take action, you must refrain from giving them the answers."[5] The experts are already in the organization.

A consultant friend did a great job of analyzing a client situation and recommending a solution. To her, it was a "no-brainer." Yet, the client did not allow her to complete the project. Why not? Because the client did not own the solution: the answers were hers, not theirs.

A manager first has to *believe* that the team *does* have the answers, and then take action based on that belief. This might require a leap of faith, especially for a manager who has created a team that depends on him for direction and answers. The next step is inviting the answers, the solutions, by asking the right questions.

When Dennis Wagner trusted that the "answers were in the room" for the federal government's organ donation initiative, his team achieved more progress in 15 months than in the previous 10 years. Because Dennis had worked with us on other projects over twelve years, he believed the answers to their challenges lay with the people who were already part of the initiative – not just his own people, but all the people involved in any way. In an unprecedented move, he and his team brought together many of the stakeholders, including hospital administrators and CEOs, many of the 59 organ procurement organizations, cardiologists and emergency room nurses, to discuss challenges and potential solutions.

At large "town hall" meetings (orchestrated "Learning Collaboratives") across the U.S., the various groups identified specific problems that they faced. Then people were asked if anyone had addressed or even solved those problems. *In every single case*, at least one person or organization (often several) had developed a solution for any particular issue that was brought up. Essentially, they had already created best-practice solutions for each of the problems, and only had to share the specifics. Thanks to people who were already involved, finding the answers was just a matter of asking the right questions. The conferences were a resounding success.

Although finding the answers was important, just as important was *who* supplied those answers. Because the stakeholders *themselves* pinpointed the solutions, they were highly motivated to make the innovations work. How could they not "buy in" to their own ideas? How could they let their own ideas fail? As Dwight D. Eisenhower was attributed to saying, "Those who plan the battle are less likely to battle the plan."

The Right Questions

A key aspect of leadership is the ability to facilitate a process of self-discovery by individuals and teams. This is very different from the traditional approach – assigning tasks or telling people what to do. In *Leadership and the New Science*, Margaret Wheatley put this type of leadership into perspective: "… we must change what we do. We will need to stop describing tasks and instead facilitate *process*. We will need to become savvy about how to build relationships, how to nurture growing, evolving things. All of us will need better skills in listening, communicating, and facilitating groups, because these are the talents that build strong relationships."[6] She emphasizes relationships because they are so critical to individual and team performance.

Notice that Dr. Wheatley twice refers to *facilitation*. Facilitation is really the art of asking the right questions, and listening to the responses. You can only effectively facilitate when you let go of the need to be the one with all the answers.

A "right" question, or Effective Question™ as we call it, is one that elicits the solutions that achieve your desired results.

How many times have you asked, "Why are we behind schedule?" and received blank stares, head scratching and muffled coughs in response? Do questions such as "Who made that decision?" provoke arguments and finger-pointing? When you ask, "Does anyone have any ideas about X?" does one person's mouth kick into hyper-drive, while others never say a word?

Like both of us in our earlier lives, odds are you've asked these kinds of questions, and endured all the negative reactions.

Why those reactions?

Because they are *ineffective* questions. Negative and backward focused, they cause people to "circle the wagons" in defensiveness instead of testing ideas and solutions. They concentrate on what's wrong, what's not working, and who's to blame. They drain energy, destroy trust, and encourage a "cover-your-butt" mentality. Instead of thinking, "What can we do to move forward?" the team member thinks, "How can I answer that question without getting blamed for the problem?" The question shifts his energy from pursuing solutions to avoiding blame.

You've probably been on the receiving end of these questions more often than you care to remember. You know from experience that they don't work.

So, if these are *in*effective questions ... what are *Effective* Questions?

Forward Focus™

Effective Questions generally employ *Forward Focus™*, a concept we introduced in Chapter 5, 'Looking at Focus,' of our previous book, *Enlightened Leadership: Getting to the Heart of Change* (go to the following website www.enleadership.com/ch5EL.pdf to read).[7] Rather than overly focusing energy and attention on what's the problem, what didn't work, and who's to blame, Forward Focus shifts more attention to what's the solution, what *did* work, who to acknowledge, and what we *can* do to move forward.

Nobody can focus on two things simultaneously. If you consistently look backward, it's impossible to focus on the tasks ahead at the same time. As illustrated by the graphic below, when the focus is on the obstacles in your path, your attention becomes mired in those obstacles instead of looking for ways to move toward your goals. That's backward focus. Forward Focus is when you continually focus on where you want to go and how to get there in order to facilitate achievement of those objectives with maximum efficiency. Along the way, of course, you certainly deal with any challenges that are keeping you from achieving the goal.

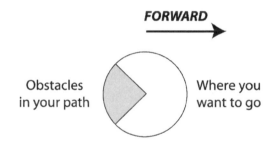

Another example of Forward vs. backward focus is the choice between "all the reasons why we cannot" accomplish a goal vs. "how we can," as illustrated on the next page. The difference is clear when we phrase the choice this way, but it's easy to slip back into the mindset of "reasons we cannot achieve the goal." From that place, that perspective, that focus, we're right – we cannot accomplish the goal. We can only accomplish it if we focus on how to do so.

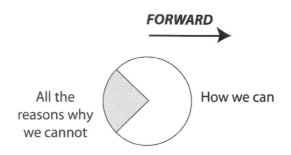

Creative thinkers – who probably make up most natural leaders – tend to focus their energy on where they want to go and keep coming back to that focus when they drift away from it. As a result, they get there much more quickly, because they continually seek solutions. Reactive thinkers often focus on obstacles and problems, getting stuck on the backward focus side. This prevents them from reaching their goals or, at minimum, slows their progress and wastes precious energy.

Forward Focus distinguishes the subtle but profound difference between focusing on problems and focusing on solutions, as illustrated on the next page. To identify a problem, you do sometimes have to put some focus on it. In order to keep moving forward, though, it is important to quickly move to the solution side and not get bogged down in what caused the problem and who was to blame. What you most want to know is how to solve it and how to prevent it from happening again.

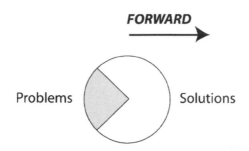

Forward Focus is a simple but powerful principle that keeps you moving toward your objectives.

Perspective from Dr. W. Edwards Deming

Renowned management expert and business consultant, the late Dr. W. Edwards Deming, corroborated the importance of the *Forward Focus* model. On an article from *Vista* magazine about his work, [8] Deming wrote in his own handwriting, "The author of this article captured in a few lines the main content of my teaching." This article was titled "Wanted: Joyful Bosses" and included the following passage:

> *"What will make for quality products and services as well as renewed leadership …? The prime requisite for achievement of any aim, including quality, is joy in work. This will require change, and management's job is to accomplish this change."*

Joy does not occur when we focus on what's *not* working – on our mistakes and failures. Instead, we facilitate joy in the workplace when we focus forward – on what *is* working, the successes we have already achieved. Because backward focus spawns defeatism, defensiveness and ill will, it can never produce joy. Forward Focus breeds joy by stimulating enthusiasm, creativity, energy, drive and collaboration – factors that can significantly increase job satisfaction, performance and productivity.

Shifting from a backward focus to a Forward Focus fundamentally alters the mindset of the people in an organization by highlighting their successes, inviting creativity and suggesting new possibilities. It's no surprise that when organizations and individuals direct more energy *toward* their objectives, they reach those objectives more quickly. Forward Focus fuels the engine of achievement while generating happier, healthier, more satisfied, and more loyal employees.

Here is an example of the value of Forward Focus. In an audit situation, a Georgia-Pacific plant was going through an ISO 9002 certification for which they had worked very hard and long. When the auditors completed their assessment, they told the director of quality, "Congratulations! You've passed the audit with such flying colors that we don't even need to do a debrief with your organization. There really aren't enough issues to mention."

The QA director responded, "We do want a debriefing. I want to get our entire organization together, and I want you to tell our people all the specific ways they did such a good job." The auditors had been so focused on finding discrepancies that they hadn't considered the value of sharing the good practices they had discovered.

Can you imagine the energy and enthusiasm in that meeting, where virtually everyone in the plant heard praise for the things they'd worked so hard to accomplish? It was powerful!

This isn't to say that you should place *zero* focus on problems. We're merely suggesting that there's greater power in shifting the *balance* toward Forward Focus. It's not about ignoring problems, but *how* we deal with problems.

How do we get people to more consistently shift their focus forward?

That's where Effective Questions come into play.

Introducing Effective Questions

Effective Questions are the most potent single leadership tool that we know. [9] It is the tool that Eli Goldratt's character, Jonah, demonstrated so effectively throughout his best-selling book, *The Goal.* [10] Jonah asked a lot of good questions, which shifted the focus of the client, which was a troubled manufacturing organization. Nothing redirects people's thinking better than a well-phrased question.

Nothing redirects people's thinking better than a well-phrased question.

Dr. George Leonard said, "A moment exists within each of us in which context suddenly shifts. And what has seemed impossible becomes possible..."

This esteemed professor's quote is about the fundamental mindset shift that Effective Questions cause.

Here is an example of that shift. Phil Schwartz experienced this shift when he spearheaded a major report to be issued under the signature of the head of his large federal agency. It was Friday morning when he suddenly realized that the introduction and context-setting chapter had not been done. The report was due at 8:00 a.m. on Monday morning, and the task seemed impossible.

Phil went to his boss, Paul, who had recently been part of a team introduced to our approach by Doug Krug. Paul completely shifted Phil's concerns by asking questions like:

- What options do you have?
- What resources are available?
- What can you do to augment resources?
- What help do you need?

Thanks to the clear thinking inspired by these questions, Phil not only met his deadline, but the entire report required only minor changes. He nailed it on the first draft! Imagine the difference in outcome if Paul's questions had been backward focused.

Looking at your own experience, suppose one of your team members is giving you all the reasons he can't make his deadline. He's stuck in a backward-focused rut. What would happen if you asked: "What would it take to finish on time?" or "What ideas do you have for getting back on track?"

Okay, maybe you'd be greeted with silence – at first. But if the person actually attempted to answer the question, he would *have to shift* his focus from "reasons why he couldn't" to "resources that he needed to get things done" or "actions that could be taken to move forward." He'd have to shift his thinking from the obstacles to the solutions, and that shift would dramatically impact the results he got.

The quality of the answers you get depends on the quality of the questions you ask.

Quality of the Answers

The quality of the answers you get depends on the quality of the questions you ask. If you're constantly hearing about all of your people's problems, check the questions you're asking. Even if they're expressing their problems *without* your prompting, you can still shift their focus using Effective Questions.

The "prime directive" of Effective Questions is to stimulate focused thought. Notice that the questions we call "effective" are open-ended. They're designed, in part, to avoid "yes" or "no" responses, which are often not helpful. Open-ended questions are asked because they invite people to elaborate without being prompted. This enhances the quality of communication by getting people to think.

One of our favorite quotes, attributed to Albert Einstein, is "All of life's answers are available, if we just knew what questions to ask." Another way of saying it is, "We will get the answers to the questions we ask – at the appropriate time." If that's true, then we must frame and ask until we have *all the answers we need*. When we ask these questions, an information-gathering process is launched that stops only when the "harvest" is complete.

For example, if you want to improve a process, you might ask the appropriate people, "What ideas do you have for improving this process?" which is very different from the more typical question "What are the problems with this process?"

If you want to enhance productivity, you ask "What could we do to make our productivity even better?" vs. "What stops us from being more productive?"

In both of the examples above, the differences are subtle but profound.

Forward Focused, open-ended questions will elicit answers that "are already in the room." Of course, we're not suggesting that Effective Questions will always produce instant results, but given time, they *will produce results*.

What questions would you most like answered right now by:

- Your team?
- An individual team member?
- A family member?
- Yourself?

Take a moment to jot down some of those questions in the space below. Open each with the words "what" or "how." This will ensure that they're open-ended questions. Make sure they are Forward Focused. Then, ask the Effective Questions of the appropriate people, and trust that the answer(s) will come – in their own time. Just do it, and see what happens.

_____

_____

_____

_____

_____

_____

_____

_____

_____

_____

Specific Effective Questions

Now that you're equipped with the concept of Effective Questions, the next chapter introduces the first of a series of specific questions to help you elicit answers to your greatest management challenges. These flexible and powerful questions make up Enlightened Leadership Solutions' Framework for Leadership. The following graphic will be used to help you keep track of where you are in the process, with each chapter being another step that builds toward the goal achievement.

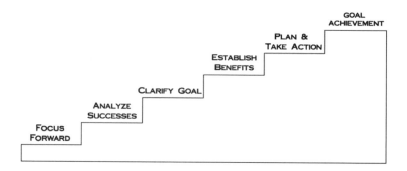

Questions to Think About

How could you use Forward Focus to help a particular situation?

What is an Effective Question that could help accomplish that?

When have you experienced a good question shifting the focus of a conversation?

Success Breeds
Success

Step 1. What is already working?

The first step of the Framework shifts people's mindsets to Forward Focus and builds creative energy in preparation for dealing with their issues, challenges or problems.

Here is an example of that first step in action. The paper manufacturing plant was in serious jeopardy with the potential for 900 people to be out of work in a Wisconsin town of 18,000. They were operating 24-7 and losing money; it seemed the more paper they made, the more money they lost, and the Fortune 500 parent company had set an expectation for closure. We were chosen as consultants for one last attempt at turning around a difficult situation.

Jennavieve Joshua was the consultant who introduced the Framework for Leadership and facilitated the management team through the process. She set the context before beginning. "I realize the challenging situation in which you find yourself. I realize everyone's job is on the line. I also know that there are many problems that you face. Knowing all that, I want to encourage you to fully participate in looking at your situation from a different perspective. I would like to use the Framework for Leadership we discussed yesterday as our guide for that. Let's experience the process, and see what happens."

She stood at a flip chart to capture input and said, "Let's begin. Realizing all the challenges you are facing, what are some of the things that are actually working? What successes are you having, no matter how small?"

The response was underwhelming. Silence was by far the strongest input. But Jennavieve had "been there before," and encouraged everyone to look at even the smallest of successes. The participants were divided into smaller groups to change the dynamics since she knew this question was a critical first step in moving toward potential solutions.

Finally, she was offered a few seemingly insignificant comments about successes – almost reluctantly. Slowly, there was a small shift in energy as individuals began to participate and more significant successes were shared. Before long, most of the team were contributing positive perspectives. The ideas generated increased buy-in for the process. A few realizations came out that were not known by the majority, yet seemed quite significant, and one specific success surprised many in the group because they didn't even know about it! More to come about that success.

The first step of the Framework for Leadership, "What is already working?" was the key to shifting the energy and focus to the *possibility* of turning around the productivity issue, becoming profitable and keeping the plant open, which was opposite from all their reasons why they were going to be shut down. This first question was the critical preparatory step to get the people Forward Focused.

The creativity pump was primed, and people were already proposing ideas about next steps, leveraging earlier successes, and achieving new goals – ultimately keeping the plant open, and saving the local economy. They were moving forward, slowly, but forward nevertheless.

"What successes are we having?" or "What is already working?"

One little type of question made all the difference. The quality of answers we get depends upon the quality of questions we ask.

Step 1 – Effective Questions

The paper plant is typical of the difference you can make when you open a meeting – any kind of meeting – with Step 1 questions, "What's already working?" "Where have we been successful? "What are our strengths?" "Where are we making progress?" These types of questions imply, "We want to focus on leveraging our current successes to achieve our goals. Backward focus, including blame games and negative thinking, has no place at the table."

This communication tool may be simple, but it has many applications, because it affects people on a variety of psychological and emotional levels, and redirects the group dynamic in positive and productive ways.

Don't mistake simplicity with simplistic or simple-minded. Some of you may be tempted to think, "This is a Pollyannaish kind of question that would *never* work in our culture." Okay. Maybe you'll receive a few blank stares or ready quips the first time you employ the approach, but this will change when people witness how Effective Questions shift the focus from backward to forward, from negative to positive, and achieve tangible results. (Note: "EQ" will be used as shorthand for Effective Question(s).)

Benefits From Step 1 Questions

A baseline of success is established. Looking at what is already successful provides a benchmark, laying the foundation from which to build. As those factors already making positive contributions are identified, it also prevents "tossing out the baby with the bathwater."

The energy level is raised. It should come as no surprise that when people start discussing their successes, they get excited. Appreciating being acknowledged for their role in shaping those successes, they also want to contribute to future achievements by making suggestions, sharing ideas, and collaborating with teammates. People leave the meeting recommitted to doing their part, and are excited about building on their successes.

Creativity is boosted. There is a natural relationship between creative energy and a positive environment, because a negative environment tends to squelch creativity, while a positive one enhances it. In a *U.S. News & World Report* article, "How to Make Yourself Happy," Holly J. Morris substantiated this link between positive emotional energy and creativity when she reported, "...positive emotions open new routes for thinking. When researchers induce positive emotions, thinking becomes more expansive and resourceful."[12]

Focus is shifted from problems to solutions. Obviously, it's important to identify what isn't working and why. We don't suggest that you ignore problems. What we *do* suggest is that a problem-focused approach is a poor way to jumpstart the creative process – the process needed to solve those problems. A Forward Focus approach to problem-solving has a very different result.

Years ago, Huck Manufacturing, a large manufacturer of components for the aerospace industry, brought their field service representatives to the New York headquarters for some meetings. Senior management had attended one of our workshops, and they decided to start the meeting by asking what was working out in the field. They didn't have a major expectation for what would happen, but it seemed like a reasonable thing to try.

They were amazed to hear about the extensive number of successes. The energy and excitement became contagious, and this one question generated discussions that lasted for more than an hour! The senior managers realized that they had never asked the service representatives to share successes. Instead, most previous interactions concentrated on problems. As they shared their successes, others experienced a revelation: someone had already solved some of their problems. The answers were in the room! It simply took one question to bring them forth.

Defensiveness is eliminated. When a discussion is opened with a backward-focused question, it suggests that people's successes are less important than their failures. In their minds, the backward focus diminishes – even invalidates – their hard work, their competence and their accomplishments. How would you feel if you labored until midnight to deliver a report to your boss on time, and her first reaction was, "Why isn't this three-hole punched? Didn't you use spell check? Who chose this font?" On the other hand, if she first complimented your hard work and commitment to making deadlines, you'd probably be less defensive if she later pointed out some different ideas or perspectives.

Resistance to change is broken down. People tend to resist change when it's forced on them without their input, and especially when their leaders imply, intentionally or not, that change is needed because something was being done wrong. We like to say, "Don't ask me to do something new or different until you first acknowledge what I'm already doing well." The first step of the Framework recognizes those successes.

In his classic book about change, *Managing Transitions: Making the Most of Change,* author William Bridges suggests that a critical part of any transition or change is to first acknowledge and honor the past.[13] Celebrating previous and current successes is a great way of doing that.

Self-confidence is built. We often ask clients, "How big a factor is self-confidence when it comes to good performance?" The answer is typically, "Huge!" That being the case, which tactic is more likely to build an employee's self-confidence: acknowledging and focusing on what she's done right, or pointing out what she's done wrong? People are more likely to believe they can achieve a major goal when you build their confidence. This is done by focusing – at the very beginning – on what they've already achieved instead of pointing out flaws and mistakes. This is especially true in group settings, where certain people make a habit of blending into the wallpaper, while others hog the microphone. When you honor the quiet people by inviting them to share successes with the group and acknowledging their value, you help build their self-confidence and encourage them to contribute ideas for the next steps.

Trust is built. When people are asked what they've done that *is* working, what they are doing *right* – it alters their self-perception. Over time, they begin to think differently about what's right with them instead of what's wrong, and as they begin to trust themselves, self-confidence is gained. They learn that they really *do* have answers. Because people with low self-confidence rarely turn things around by themselves, it's important for you – as leader – to help shift their attitudes by using the "what's already working" type of question, which can help clear up emotional and mental gridlock. Trust is also built in those asking the questions when there is clarity that the questions are not threatening.

The complainers are disarmed. In addition to building trust, the first step of the Framework empowers your innovative thinkers, while disarming the complainers in your group – the people who see nothing but half-empty glasses. Government organizations sometimes call the latter "CAVE people" (Citizens Against Virtually Everything), and they are usually very vocal about how bad everything is, what all of the problems are and who's to blame, and it's never them! Fortunately, the EQ hands the microphone to those who want to look for solutions and strengths, and away from the negative people. This gives you an opportunity to hear from more innovative and effective people, and invites complainers to look at a new perspective – the Forward Focus side of things.

Modifying the Question to Fit the Situation

There are as many ways to phrase the Step 1 Effective Question as there are applications for it. Here is one real-world example.

Michelle Brown, customer service manager at a large plastics manufacturer, put a new spin on the Step 1 Effective Question as soon as she returned to work from a session with one of our facilitators. "Michelle, we've got an irate customer," said her colleagues. "Here's the information. You've got to call this guy!"

She thought, "I'd like to start by asking the customer what's already working, but, to say the least, that could come off as self-serving. How can I re-word the question and still take advantage of the concept?" The solution came to her quickly.

When she phoned the customer, she immediately gave him the opportunity to vent about the problem – a key part of her process. Once his negativity had dissipated, she asked, "Mr. Thompson, what have other vendors done in this situation that's worked well for you?" A stunned Mr. Thompson collected his thoughts and answered her. Then Michelle said, "OK. If we did that within the next few days, would it satisfy you?" He said it would. She implemented the solution and gained a very satisfied customer. The key to the turnaround was a nicely adapted "what's working?" question.

As the previous example demonstrates how you can adapt the Step 1 Effective Question for a specific situation, there are many other applications in addition to project meetings and customer service activities. Here are a few additional examples:

- *Performance Evaluation.* "What are some of your biggest strengths, and how have you utilized them during the last year?" "What are some of the successes you've had this year? What else?"

- *Performance Management and Enhancement.* During a training session at the Orange County Sheriff's Department, cadets were asked, "What did you do well at the simulated crime scene?" This forced the cadets to analyze and evaluate their performance from a positive perspective, and created openness for the rest of the discussion.

- *Conflict Resolution.* "What do you and Fred agree on?" "Where have you found common ground in the past?" "What do you respect or admire about the other person?"

- *Building Collaboration and Teamwork.* "What are you already doing together that works well?" "What strengths do your teammates bring to the process?" We were involved in a situation between a manager and her team in which nobody had anything good to say about her. Prior to facilitating a session between the employees and their manager, we asked each employee to think about what he or she sincerely appreciated about this woman's leadership. Every person found something good to say in the meeting, which set the stage for the next important part of the conversation.

- *Business Plan Review.* "No matter how small, what aspects of your plan are working so far? What else? Of everything you have tried so far, what parts are creating some success?"

- *Tracking Others' Successes.* "What are other organizations doing successfully in similar circumstances?" Encouraging people to research similar situations inside and outside their own industry for successful practices opens the potential for fresh ideas.

Regardless of the situation or circumstances, the primary benefit of the Step 1 EQ is that it causes you to focus on what you did well, not what you did wrong. This applies to individual, as well as group efforts. You can ask *yourself* these questions to stimulate your own creativity and problem-solving abilities.

Over the years, we've received calls from many clients who have spent entire meetings focusing on just the first step of the Framework, because the question sparked so much learning and energy that resulted in solutions, which ultimately impacted progress.

The first step Effective Question is *that* effective, because success breeds continued success.

- **What is already working?**
- **What successes are we having?**
- **Where do we agree?**
- **What are some things you appreciate about the situation?**
- **What have we done successfully in similar situations in the past?**

- What do you appreciate or respect about the person (or relationship)?
- What went well this week?

These are all examples of the first step of the Framework for Leadership. In the next chapter, you will discover how to build on your successes with the second step of the Framework.

Questions to Think About

What is a backward focused situation in which a "What's already working?" question could shift the focus back toward a solutions-orientation?

How, specifically, would you word the question to keep it Forward Focused and open-ended?

Getting to the Root
Cause ...of Success

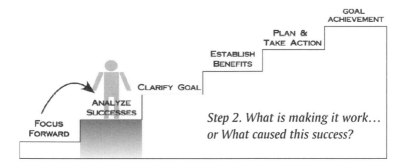

ANALYZE SUCCESSES

FOCUS FORWARD

CLARIFY GOAL

ESTABLISH BENEFITS

PLAN & TAKE ACTION

GOAL ACHIEVEMENT

Step 2. What is making it work... or What caused this success?

T
he intention of the second step of the Framework for Leadership is to learn from successes so they can be replicated. It also builds more creative energy while acknowledging people at a more detailed level for how they caused successes.

The "What makes it work?" question is designed to facilitate a root-cause analysis of a success – yours or some-one else's. If you hope to duplicate and build on prior achievements, it makes sense to learn *why* something suc-ceeded. Unfortunately, most managers are fixated on understanding the causes of failure. They become experts in the field of incompetence, but remain unconscious about what drives their organization's competence.

Earlier in chapter 2, we outlined how Dennis Wagner and his team (including, but not limited to Ginny McBride, John Scanlon, Dr. Frank Zampinella, Jade Perdue and Helen Bottenfield) led an initiative that generated a stun-ning increase in the number of organs available for trans-plant. They did so by finding "the answers in the room." Exactly *how* they found those answers brings us to Step 2 of the Framework.

When Wagner took the reins, he noticed that only about 200 out of 5,800 hospitals were achieving adequate dona-tion rates where about 50% of potential donors actually donated their organs. If every hospital were to achieve that rate, nobody – *nobody* – would die for lack of an organ. At that time, 88,000 people were on waiting lists, and 17 people died each day in need of an organ. Wagner realized that the issue wasn't a lack of organs, but an inefficient donor system. Daily, people with usable organs were buried alongside those who might have lived – had they received one of those organs.

From Unconscious Competence...

One of his first steps as project leader was to ask his team, "What are these 200 most successful hospitals doing differently?" Their initial answer was, "We don't know. We've been trying to find out what the other 5,600 hospitals are doing wrong." Let's be clear. These were not bad people. They were just stuck in the "find the problem and fix it" mindset, which is so easy to do in our society. Having worked with Effective Questions (EQ's) for years, Wagner clearly understood the value of building on successes, not problems.

In addition, there were two cities with donation rates much higher than the average, Houston, Texas and Madison, Wisconsin. Dennis contacted their Organ Procurement Organizations (OPO's) to discover why they were so successful. Once again, the response was, "We don't know." These two OPO's were simply doing what they normally did, and it happened to be working. They didn't realize that other OPO's were not as successful or that they had pioneered a unique model – until they were asked.

In one specific example that was unique, the OPO coordinators were assigned to specific hospitals. They actually remained on site at the primary hospitals on a 24/7 basis, instead of having to be paged when needed. This allowed them to develop relationships with families early in life-threatening circumstances, making it much easier to ask for organ donations.

By asking the right questions, Wagner's team discovered their model, and introduced it to Organ Procurement Organizations throughout the country using the "Learning Collaborative" model. Utilizing this and other successful practices has helped produce amazing results in very little time. Since the collaboratives began in September of 2003, monthly results have continued to set a new record in donated organs compared to the same month the previous year.

Imagine the increase in excitement as team members in various hospitals and OPO's learned how and why things were working elsewhere. That information gave them answers to long-standing problems, which generated tremendous enthusiasm and boosted everyone's creativity.

Although the specifics of the donation program are fascinating, what's more important to understand is the *process* that created this ongoing success – a process that begins when you ask the Step 2 Effective Question:

What is the cause of this success?
or **What, specifically, makes it work?**

...To Conscious Competence

The goal of Step 2 of the Framework, therefore, is to bring people from unconscious competence, not knowing why they are successful, to conscious competence, which is being fully aware of why they are successful. If we don't know why we've succeeded in the past, we can't learn from those successes, and we certainly can't transfer this knowledge to others.

Sadly, this concept and behavior is frequently "missing in action" in corporate America. When we achieve a success, our tendency, at best, is to acknowledge the victory and say, "Next." One large computer company prides itself on "celebrating for a nanosecond" before moving on. If they are moving on so quickly, you can bet that they are not taking time to learn from their successes. They're far less likely to consistently repeat their successes if they don't take time to understand their causes.

Too many leaders hit the "red alert button," and assemble all hands to analyze problems whenever they occur. Too few call meetings to analyze their most recent successes. A high-tech laser-development firm based in Lexington, Massachusetts was typical. Years ago, in one of our consulting sessions, management had the revelation that whenever they lost a sale, everyone spent days poring over every aspect of why they'd lost. When they were awarded a project, however, everyone cheered and then forgot about it. They had *no idea* what they'd done to win certain bids, but knew in detail what they'd done to lose others. They realized they had it backwards. The real opportunity was in analyzing the successes so they could be consistently repeated.

In the last chapter, we pointed to a Wisconsin paper mill that was facing closure. When "What is already working?" was facilitated, people were surprised that one particular shift, using one particular paper machine out of five, was more productive than all the rest. Jennavieve, the facilitator, couldn't wait to ask, "What is that one team doing differently to be more productive?" (Notice that this is a variant of "What makes it work?") The answer to that single question was not well known, but when the details surfaced, it showed the management team how to substantially improve productivity, take the plant to profitability and keep it open.

Most of the plant *did not know* what that one team was doing to be more productive. Imagine the impact when 14 other teams implemented the strategy that was working so well for that team. Bottom-line: they stayed in business, saved their jobs and the local economy! Not bad for a simple little leadership process.

Missed Opportunity

Ed Oakley had dinner with a number of Human Resource Directors who lived near the border of North and South Carolina and met monthly to share ideas. He was really impressed when they started their meeting by sharing a success that each of them had experienced over the previous month.

Ed was particularly interested when one person shared that he had led a very successful rollout of a new health insurance program. He said that buy-in was very high, and you could tell by his voice how excited he was. Ed was eager to learn how he'd accomplished such a great success, as Ed had rarely heard of a successful rollout of any new insurance program. Even if the new program was really better, people tended to be skeptical and suspicious of management's intentions.

Ed waited for the next question to be asked, "What did you do to create such an extraordinary success?" but no one asked! They just applauded the manager and moved to the next person. That is so typical of how we don't take time to learn from the successes we experience or hear about. We throw away many learning opportunities.

Step 2 of the Framework is very important and can be phrased in many ways:

- **What made it work? What is making it work?**
- **What, specifically, caused the success?**
- **To what do you attribute that success? What else?**
- **What did they do to accomplish that win?**
- **What made this situation different, so that the success was much greater?**
- **What did you do differently this time vs. last time to create a higher level of success?**
- **What did they do on a similar project that solved or prevented that problem?**

These are variations of the second-level question, which can be adapted to fit any number of situations – project meetings, product evaluations, analyzing general successes, marketing reviews, sales successes, and so forth. The wording isn't particularly important, so long as the focus is on understanding the details that led to the successes.

Build a Learning Organization

What you have is the opportunity to build a learning organization, because when people are running on solutions-oriented questions, learning happens naturally. When competence becomes conscious, it can be documented and duplicated.

When competence becomes conscious, it can be documented and duplicated.

Here is an example with which you might relate. Some of you may lead – or work with – sales departments where a relative handful of "superstars" account for most of the business. Because the success of these salespeople is usually attributed to "raw talent" or "intuition," little or no effort is made to identify and catalog their techniques, talents, activities, actions and strategies. No one picks their brains for tools that could be taught to others. To be sure, some successes probably *do* stem from their instincts and talents, which are nontransferable; however, other skills, actions and strategies *are* transferable. By using Step 2 of the Framework, you can identify the transferable competencies, and construct a process that can be employed by many others. You could also develop a hiring process that seeks to pinpoint those talents and skills in prospective employees.

Why Was this Meeting a Success?

Let's say you've just finished a productive meeting – whether scheduled or impromptu. Why not conduct a "post-game" analysis? "Hey folks, how did you feel about this meeting today?" If people agreed that it was a good meeting, ask further, "What do you think made this meeting better? What did we do to make it successful?" Keep asking, "What else? What else? What else?" Drill down to the root causes of success until you locate and understand them. Odds are you'll discover some tools or ideas that will come in handy for future meetings.

The same goes for breakthroughs. If your team has just had a big win, learn from it. We often celebrate breakthroughs, but how often do we take time to dig down and understand how they came about? There are reasons for those successes. Be sure to understand what they are.

Ed did a talk in the Midwest for 95 communication company employees who had just completed a very successful IT (Information Technology) project. They were taking the day off from normal work to celebrate an amazing success with a large, challenging project. Having lunch with the project leader after the talk, Ed – noting the huge success – asked the manager, "How much time did you spend at the end of the project to really understand what you and your people did to cause such an impressive success?" She was silent for a few moments, then said enthusiastically, "That's a great idea!" – which meant they had not done it!

Whatever the situation or venue, find solutions by building a learning collaborative like the one used by the organ donation initiative – a model that brings people together to learn from one another. Here, the focus is not on scrutinizing problems, but on learning about successful practices. When you ask what made it work, you begin searching for a common element: what someone or a team of people did well. But don't stop there. Use the process to probe deeper, to understand exactly *what* they did to be successful.

Everyone appreciates it when you tell them "good job," but often they aren't aware of what critical factors led to their success – *until you get them to really think about it.* That's why everyone benefits from Step 2 of the Framework.

That's the root cause of why this question succeeds.

What made it work? or

What caused the success?

Questions to Think About

What recent successes could be more valuable by better understanding what caused them?

What question might you ask?

Getting on the Right Track

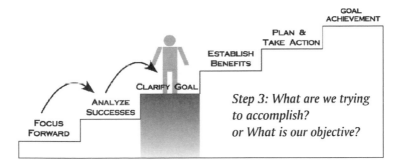

GOAL ACHIEVEMENT

PLAN & TAKE ACTION

ESTABLISH BENEFITS

CLARIFY GOAL

ANALYZE SUCCESSES

FOCUS FORWARD

Step 3: What are we trying to accomplish? or What is our objective?

S tep 3 of the Framework for Leadership establishes a clear goal, vision, objective or mission to gain or assure alignment of the team for focusing its efforts.

Perhaps you can relate to an example. The meeting has been an unqualified success so far. You've employed Step 1 and Step 2 of the Framework to determine *what's already working* and *what caused those successes*. You've jump-started your team's energy, creativity and enthusiasm, and everyone seems to be on the right track – bursting with ideas. You stand, arrange the papers in front of you, and ask, "Is everyone clear on the objective?" Heads nod all around the room.

"Great," you think, "it's time to rock and roll!"

Uh, …not so fast.

Are you *sure* that everyone's clear on the objective? Do they all see it the same? Are they fully aligned? You won't know for certain unless you ask the right questions – unless you keep asking.

Don't be fooled by heads nodding. It's a good bet that some people are *anything but clear* about the objective. Worse, they might be clear in their own minds, but their ideas may diverge from the team's real goal, or they may have misunderstood you. For example, you may have said, "Let's go!" – meaning let's get going on our process, but they heard, "Let's go!" – meaning let's leave. And sometimes the stated objective is so vague that nobody could ever agree on *how* to achieve it, let alone *when* it was achieved. It's important to have everyone discuss the objectives to assure clarity.

If there is any alignment issue, this is the step where it will come out. It might come in the form of disagreement, or it might come in lack of energy or participation. If that happens, you must sideline the process until you determine and clear any issues. Chapter 10 will provide some guidance on how to deal with this situation.

The Third Step of the Framework

Several years ago, *USA Today* reported from a survey the main reasons that teams fail, with the number one reason being unclear goals and number two, *changing goals.*

In our consulting work with clients, we often distribute a discovery questionnaire to participants in advance of our interventions, processes or events, asking both managers and their subordinates to define their current objectives. Time after time, management lists one set of goals while the employees list another. People on different rungs of the organizational ladder often have different perspectives about directions and objectives. The typical response from lower levels is, "It would really help if we had clear direction," while the response from higher levels is usually, "Our direction is very clear."

Step 3 of the Framework, therefore, is to ask:

"What is our objective?" or

"What are we trying to accomplish?"

This is an essential step for getting people onto the right track and moving in the same direction. After all, you can't expect everyone to arrive at the same destination if you haven't agreed where it is.

Why Isn't This Step 1 Instead of Step 3?

Sometimes we hear, "Why isn't this question the first step of the Framework, instead of the third? It seems like you need to *start* with the objective." There is a certain amount of truth to that. To begin using the 5-step Framework, you have to have some idea of the objective you're dealing with, and you establish that upfront as the context for why you're using this process. After building the creative energy, though, we have found it extremely valuable to go back and look at the objective with new eyes. Often the result is an entirely different and more meaningful understanding of the objective. Gaining alignment with a clear, shared goal is much easier when the foundation has been set with the first two Framework steps.

Let's look at an example of the importance of a clear objective. A surgical manufacturing division of a Fortune 500 company was installing a new enterprise-wide computer system. The project team was struggling with priorities. Because the project would impact everyone in the manufacturing environment, the project leader, Terri Martin, also controller of the facility, used the Framework for Leadership to plan the transition process. When the team reached Step 3, however, they experienced a revelation. With the question, "What is our objective?" three different conflicting objectives were uncovered, which had been put forth by three different stakeholders. They realized that the conflicting goals were making it difficult to establish priorities for moving forward. Their first action, then, was to resolve these conflicting goals with the stakeholders. Then, with the new clarity, they were able to focus on the appropriate priorities.

Avoidance and Distraction

In the absence of a clearly defined goal, people often shift to an "avoidance focus." But when the focus is on avoiding mistakes, we actually gravitate toward those mistakes. Without any concrete *do's*, we steer straight for the *do nots*. Avoiding doesn't work! What we try to avoid is the very thing our attention and action go toward.

> **In the absence of a clearly defined goal, people often shift to an "avoidance focus."**

There is a natural tendency for people to shift to this avoidance focus – avoid mistakes, avoid being late, avoid problems, avoid risk. Because of the natural tendency to focus on what we want to avoid, leadership needs to pull the team back to the actual goal. Therefore, it is vital that goals and objectives are stated positively. The goal of "increasing sales" is not the same as "don't lose sales." Step

3 of the Framework helps bring us back on track and keep us there. "What is our goal here?" "What are we trying to accomplish?"

It's also natural for people to become distracted in the workplace. We're not referring to the chronic goof-off who plays computer games or surfs the Internet instead of working, but the average person who gets distracted by various tasks, phone calls, personal issues, emails, interruptions, etc. They lose clarity about what's important, because these distractions cause them to lose sight of what they're doing and why. They become more reactive than proactive. Instead of running on the question, "What's my objective?" or "What is the best use of my time?" or "What are my priorities?" a person might think, "How do I get through the day?" or "How could I possibly get all this done?" He makes decisions based on the moment instead of the stated objective and disconnects from the larger goal.

When Ed Tate, senior facilitator and speaker, approached the final rounds of the Toastmasters world speaking competition, it seemed *everybody* was giving him advice about what *not* to do, and he was listening! Then it suddenly struck him, "Wait a minute. I don't want to focus on what *not* to do. That's like focusing on the very thing I don't want. I need to focus on what I *do* want." He shifted his strategy and started asking previous winners what they had done to become champions.

Using the question, "What did you do to win?" he discovered what he needed to know about how to succeed. The answer wasn't about what *not* to do. It was about what *to* do. Now he had a clear vision of what it took to win, and he did. Ed Tate became Toastmasters 2000 World Champion, winning over 20,000 contestants! He is confident that a significant factor was shifting focus away from "what not to do" and toward "what he wanted to do."

Forgetting the Real Goal

Here's a classic example of what happens when we lose sight of our ultimate objective. And it's a valuable reminder of why it's important to bring people back to the objective with, "What are we trying to accomplish?" People become so wedded to short-term objectives that they sometimes lose sight of the big picture by focusing on the immediate issue and forgetting about the larger goal.

We once worked with the executives of a major West Coast hospital, who were upset because many managers were not conducting their annual employee reviews in a timely manner. The executive team had brainstormed the problem and proposed everything from posting the offenders' names on a bulletin board to docking their pay. Our facilitator, Jonette Crowley, asked the executive team,

"What's your goal?" Their response: "To get everybody to perform the evaluations on time." She drilled deeper: "What's the purpose of that?" (This was another way of asking "What's the real goal?") After each response, Jonette kept asking, "What's the purpose of that ... and that?" until they finally admitted, "The ultimate goal is to improve the performance of our people."

There it was! Performance enhancement was the ultimate purpose, not timely submission of evaluations. The short-term objective was a tool for achieving a larger goal. Once the larger goal was clear, a big issue surfaced regarding the performance evaluation instrument. The evaluation format was actually hampering performance! Because the reviews forced managers to pigeonhole their people and look for weaknesses, many reacted passively by not conducting them. The executives had lost sight of the ultimate objective. As a consequence, they were not dealing with the real issue. When this became clear, the suggestion was made to create an annual review process that focused on enhancing the employee's strengths and behaviors to help them move forward, not dwelling on criticism of past mistakes.

Your People Have the Answers

Achieving clarity around an objective is critical, but it's just as important to gain a high level of buy-in. Although your people may be clear about the goal, you won't accomplish much without their ownership. Therefore, it's a good idea to get people involved in helping to establish the objective – whenever possible. If everyone has a say in determining the objective, you are more assured of buy-in.

Although your people may be clear about the goal, you won't accomplish much without their ownership.

As an example, in the late '70's when Ed Oakley was still a district manager at Hewlett Packard, he asked a colleague named Lee Blackstone for advice on how to set quotas for the salespeople on his team. Lee suggested that Ed assemble his salespeople in a room and tell them what the quota would be for the entire team. Then, the team would have the rest of the day to figure out the individual targets, which had to add up to the district total. In other words, leave it up to the team members to establish individual goals. Of course, they knew if they were unable to accomplish the task by the end of the day, quotas would be assigned to them.

Ed saw nothing to lose and put the idea in motion. The results were amazing. Near the end of the day, the sales-people approached Ed and said: "OK, we're ready to talk." Ed sat down with the team, and each person declared his individual quota – each person took responsibility and ownership for his goal.

Ed asked how each person felt about his quota and, in every case, the person responded by saying that the targets were fair and reasonable. Some people assigned them-selves lower quotas than Ed would have given, but others accepted higher targets. In most cases, the senior people took on more responsibility to show their commitment to the team and their support of the new people.

The bottom-line: allowing the salespeople to establish their own specific and measurable objectives created a tre-mendous level of ownership. The result was a very success-ful year for the team.

A Minor Shift in Objective
Can Make a Big Difference

In order for a major U.S. manufacturer of special oph-thalmic lenses used in cataract surgery to expand its pro-duction capabilities, management needed to transfer technology for building the devices from its U.S. manufacturing division to a European division. We were brought in to work with the team, which we'll call XYZ Transfer Team.

We made excellent progress until we asked the team to clarify their objective. At that point, there was a discernible shift – as if the energy had dropped for some reason. Sensing something wrong, Ed queried the participants: "There's something about this objective that isn't clear or that some people don't like. What's going on? What is the skunk under the table that no one is mentioning?"

After a couple of minutes, some people from the U.S. division opened up. *Transferring* manufacturing knowledge and capability to Europe implied that the U.S. facility could potentially be closed – that 600 American employees might eventually lose their jobs. However unlikely it was, the possibility existed, and there were some people back at the U.S. plant who were concerned.

No wonder there was an energy drain! Who would enthusiastically pursue an objective that might cost him his job?

Ed asked the senior managers present if the intention was to eventually lay off the American workers? "No," they responded quickly, "not at all." It wasn't about taking jobs from one plant and giving them to another. It was about expansion. In this high-growth market for the XYZ product, the company needed additional manufacturing capacity – two factories instead of one. What came to light was that this was not really the XYZ Transfer Team, but the XYZ *Expansion* Team. The sense of relief was significant. The misunderstanding that had surfaced through the right questions was resolved, and the true objective was clarified. There was high buy-in for the real goal.

Step 3 of the Framework offers a great opportunity to demonstrate leadership through Effective Questions. Having unleashed your people's energy and creativity with Steps 1 and 2, you now harness those assets, and direct them toward accomplishing goals that are both clear and specific. Once you generate enthusiasm and buy-in for the goal, the journey ahead will require less time and less wasted effort. In many cases, your people will don the engineer's cap and take responsibility for steering the train.

Of course, it's not always possible to achieve buy-in by allowing people to establish their own objectives. Sometimes the objective is passed down from above, or you are so clear about the objective that you're not open to discussing options. In that case, you'll need to find alternate routes to buy-in. We will address that situation in the next chapter.

6

Why Are We Doing This Anyway?

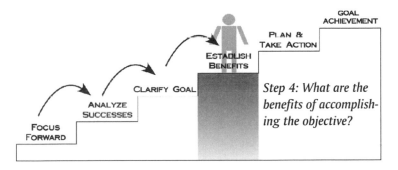

GOAL ACHIEVEMENT

PLAN & TAKE ACTION

ESTABLISH BENEFITS

CLARIFY GOAL

ANALYZE SUCCESSES

FOCUS FORWARD

Step 4: What are the benefits of accomplishing the objective?

S tep 4 of the Framework facilitates commitment to, and ownership of, the goal by those who are critical to implementing it. When benefits for accomplishing the goal are clear for all stakeholders: customers, shareholders, the company, the department, the team, and the individuals involved, buy-in is high and success is optimized.

By asking, "What are the benefits of accomplishing our objective?" the fourth step of the Framework seeks to uncover everyone's incentives, or lack of incentives, for achieving a goal. When individuals find their own positive answers to the question, they acquire a personal stake in the outcome and will gladly focus energy, attention and resources on the tasks at hand. Without a clear, concrete stake in the outcome, motivation will vary based on each person's "accidental clarity" – her innate ability to sense why the mission is important. Clear, intelligible answers to the Step 4 question establish personal and team buy-in.

When people respond to the benefits question, they reveal their true reasons for investing in the goal – their underlying motivations. By so doing, they will either validate, or invalidate, the objective as being worthy of their time and resources. Every person who recognizes the project's benefits lends credibility to its accomplishment. Every individual's buy-in enhances the project's significance and validity, thus providing the greatest possibility for excellent results.

A clear example arose in our own company. For seven years, we promoted and delivered a public seminar called "Making Managers into Leaders" in six to twelve cities across the U.S. every month. It cost a lot of money to market and deliver these seminars, with most of the expenses occurring before the events took place. Unfortunately, we were averaging only 34% in upfront collection of fees, so we had to pay extraordinary expenses with little income to offset them. The result – we had a *big* cash flow problem.

Jonathon James was managing the public seminar effort, including the call center responsible for registering people and collecting payments. We needed to raise upfront collections to 75-80%, so Jon and George Metanias, our president, facilitated a meeting using the Framework for Leadership to focus on solving the problem.

When the goal step was reached, they asked, "What do you think you could accomplish if you really put your mind to it? What goal might you be able to achieve in terms of increasing the percentage of upfront collections?" Immediately, one person asked them, "If we really make a big improvement, how might we get rewarded?" Realizing this would help the company significantly, George said that we would pay a bonus if the numbers were really good.

Knowing there was a payoff for them, the employees huddled in the conference room to come up with their own goal. When they were ready, they brought Jon and George back inside. "We think we can do 90% upfront collections!" The senior managers were stunned, and told them that achieving that number would earn a significant bonus and even specified what the bonus would be. They were delighted to accept the challenge, though Jon and George weren't very optimistic.

Within two months, they were averaging 95% upfront collections, which was unheard of in the public seminar business! The company was much healthier, and the call center team was jubilant.

Costs vs. Benefits

Basically, this Effective Question prompts every stakeholder to run a cost-benefit analysis – if only in their head. Based on this, everyone will attempt to gauge: (A) if the goal offers any worthwhile personal benefits; and (B) whether the overall mission is likely to succeed. Ideally, you're looking for a positive response to (A) *and* (B) to maximize your chances of success.

Suppose you've just facilitated the planning process for a major project that will take a lot of time, money, resources and effort. The group is clear on the objective. Now you ask the question, "What are the benefits for the customer, the company, this division, this team and each of you as individuals?" Suppose there aren't a lot of benefits, or the benefits do not clearly offset the effort and investment required? What is the message?

Realistically, the message is that you'd better take another serious look at this project. It might not be worth doing! Put simply, if people can't think of clear benefits for their efforts, then the goal, or how it is understood, needs to be revisited.

Harnessing Different Motivations

One advantage of this process is that it helps to clarify and quantify the benefits to everyone. It forces you to redefine the abstract as the concrete, leaving no room for vague or fuzzy promises. Of course, you may have to dig deeper to unearth everyone's true motivations. But in many cases, repeating Step 4, "What's the value/benefit of that?" is sufficient. When someone says, "If this works, it would be fun," we ask something like, "What's the value to you, *personally?*" This prompts people to reveal what's important to them at a deeper level. Or you might simply ask, "How would you quantify that benefit?"

His answer tells you what is most important to him because each person may have entirely different motivations. Does one person want to know about return on investment? Is another concerned about the consequences to the organization's people? Someone might care most about an initiative's effect on customers, while another wants to know how it fits into the corporate culture. One common, but often unspoken, motivation is: "How will this project make me look?"

None of these motivations is bad or good. They're merely different examples of primary motivators. Asking

"What are the benefits from your perspective?" can tell you a lot about an individual's motivation. Be aware, however, that a person's response might *not contain the whole truth*. Some people won't feel comfortable discussing which parts of the project matter most to them.

Not to worry. Either way, this scenario is good news:

- It doesn't matter what they say. It only matters that they get in touch with their personal benefits – that they process the question for themselves.

- The focus they put into their responses will often tell you whether they've shared all of their underlying motivations or just some. You can also pick up hints as to which motivators are most important.

Buy-in from All Stakeholders

Many managers are so focused on getting buy-in from subordinates that they forget about the need for buy-in from colleagues and superiors. Although initiatives are frequently passed down from above, there are occasions when your team will want to implement projects of their own design and will need approval and support from upper management. In those instances, there's a need to "sell" the benefits that matter most to management. And what matters most to senior managers is usually what matters most to customers, shareholders, strategic partners, departments, vendors, etc.

Before posing the Step 4 EQ, "What are the benefits of accomplishing our objective?" to upper management, therefore, it makes sense to *first* pose the question on behalf of the other stakeholders. When you facilitate a what's-the-benefit discussion, you need to determine the benefits for *all* stakeholders – customers, shareholders, the company, this department, the team and each individual involved.

In our experience, we find such discussions are most effective when they move from the "outside" to the "inside." In other words, we first lead a discussion of how the project will benefit customers – those most outside the organization. Second, we address the benefits to shareholders or employees throughout the organization. And third, we discuss the department and team most directly involved in implementing the program.

Because the "outside-in" approach demonstrates that many entities will gain value from the project – customers, the whole company, the department, your team – it serves as a reminder that it's permissible for us, as individuals, to feel that we deserve some benefits, too. Asking a subordinate, "What is the benefit for you, personally?" too soon might produce hesitation and concern, because he may not want to appear "selfish." But when it becomes clear that so many different stakeholders will benefit from the project, you're likely to receive more answers from your team members, and they will be based on honesty, which will lead to a highly motivated team. Perhaps a more effective way of asking the question to individuals is, "What will it do for you, personally?"

One example of the true power of buy-in involved an information technology project at a major insurance company. The project manager had done everything he knew to get everyone focused on completing the project within the 30-day deadline, but it was clear they wouldn't come close to meeting that target.

Doug Krug brought the team together to introduce the Framework for Leadership, the concepts and ideas behind it, and how it fit into the context of their project. He then facilitated the Framework to create clear action plans for completing the project on time.

The first two steps went reasonably well. He captured numerous successes, as well as who, and what, contributed to those successes. When he got to Step 3, "What is the objective?" the goal seemed clear, but Doug noticed a strange quiet in the room, almost lackadaisical. Unsure of what to do about it, he proceeded to Step 4, "What are the benefits of accomplishing the objectives – to the outside customers, the shareholders, the company, the division, the team, each of us as individuals?"

The feeling in the room was subdued as people shared typical reasons how the various stakeholders would benefit, and how they would each personally benefit from finishing on time. Something was missing, and everyone knew it. There was a skunk in the room that wasn't being identified. Finally, out of frustration, the project manager blurted out, "...and you get to keep your jobs!" People chuckled at first, but then they realized that he was serious.

"What is that supposed to mean?" someone asked.

"I shouldn't have said that," the manager said more quietly, "but there is a strong rumor that we are being watched very closely on this project, and if we don't finish on time, our roles could be outsourced to another company."

They were stunned at this message, and as discussions continued, they realized that no one had even thought the deadline was serious. There had been no buy-in for the deadline. This new information – the possibility of being outsourced – fueled a completely new focus by the entire team. Suddenly, there was 100% focus on what it would take to finish the project on time. Failure was no longer an option. *That is the real power of buy-in.*

The rest of the story ... they finished the project within the deadline – a small miracle.

We have the opportunity to gain the power of buy-in and ownership when we ask Step 4 questions like:

What are the benefits of accomplishing our objective?
What is the value for the company?

What will it do for you, personally?

What are some of the hidden benefits that might not be so obvious?

Now that we have strong ownership for the objective, we move to Step 5, the action planning phase of the Framework.

A Question to Think About:

What is a situation in which commitment is half-hearted that might value from facilitating a discussion of the benefits for all stakeholders for accomplishing the objective?

Closing the Gap ...
the Solution Step

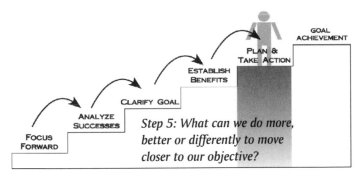

GOAL ACHIEVEMENT

PLAN & TAKE ACTION

ESTABLISH BENEFITS

CLARIFY GOAL

ANALYZE SUCCESSES

FOCUS FORWARD

Step 5: What can we do more, better or differently to move closer to our objective?

S tep 5 of the Framework for Leadership is the Action Plan, which includes accountability and measurement. Steps 1-4 have been preparation for this step.

Dave Malenfant, global supply-chain vice president for a worldwide company headquartered in Texas, had a problem: Product lead times in Europe were unacceptable. For months, his team had addressed the challenge without much improvement. Having been introduced to the

Framework for Leadership in a management development workshop, Dave decided to gather the European managers together in Belgium, and use the Enlightened Leadership Framework to address the issue.

Since this was a new process to them, it wasn't surprising that the team started slowly, since each individual was trying to determine their role and gauge whether it was safe to contribute. But by the time they reached Step 5, which is the action step of the Framework, the room was charged with energy and creativity. Participation was at a very high level even though team members were impatient to "get to the solution." Dave knew, however, that it was important to lay the groundwork before tackling the situation head-on. He knew the value of acknowledging the team for their successes and achievements before he invited them to do even better.

As soon as the question was asked, "What can we do more, better or differently to move closer to our objective?" one manager devised a simple, yet brilliant, solution to the . It involved a clever way to reprioritize the order-taking process. This one idea alone, which never came up during the previous months of traditional problem-solving and brainstorming, saved 20 days of lead time for the European operations. The key to eliciting that elegant solution was to go through *all* the steps and gain the benefits of each. The process developed creative energy, trust and an openness resulting in ideas for solutions across the multi-national organization.

Beginning the Action Plan

Step 5 marks the beginning of solution implementation. All the previous steps of the process have been to prepare us for this step. Frankly, if we could go straight to this step, and generate sufficient creativity, trust and openness, we would! Experience has shown us, however, that moving directly into brainstorming and problem-solving doesn't often work. We must first prepare the soil and plant the seeds before we can expect to reap the harvest. The first two steps represent that preparation and planting. Also part of the preparation is clarifying the objective, Step 3, and developing the ownership, Step 4. The action plan, Step 5, is the beginning of the harvest. This step utilizes the creativity and enthusiasm generated through the first four steps, to solve the problem.

We must first prepare the soil and plant the seeds before we can expect to reap the harvest.

"What can we do more, better or differently to move closer to our objective?" gets everyone involved in the solution. It invites them to assume personal leadership and be part of the solution, not just part of the problem. It encourages people to share their ideas, knowledge and creativity, and it honors people for their contributions.

The action plan establishes a true team approach to meeting the challenge. Everyone is encouraged to participate, and as they do, they almost always develop more effective solutions. As they look at what can be done better or differently, notice they are identifying what needs to change – a more palatable, less threatening way of looking at the problem. As the action plan evolves, it moves them toward specific tasks and appropriate accountability.

A Continuous Process of Improvement

It's important to realize that it may neither be realistic nor necessary to solve the entire problem in one huge bite. We just need to get started toward a solution by progressively biting off chewable chunks of the problem, or gap, to better deal with them. When we approach challenges from this perspective, we ensure that our people won't feel overwhelmed by large or difficult issues.

When the insurance regional claim center mentioned in Chaptproblemer 1 was operating at a customer service rating of 58%, achieving a rating anywhere near 90%

seemed impossible. So, when management reached Step 3 of the Framework, "What are we trying to accomplish?" they knew not to set a huge, numerical goal. Instead, they let their people set the goal. When the claim center team established a goal of optimizing their customer service rating, they realized this would require an ongoing, continuous improvement process, and impressive numbers would not be created overnight.

The various teams started their periodic progress review meetings by celebrating the successes they'd had in customer service improvement since the last meeting (Step 1) and pinpointing what had contributed to those successes (Step 2). Then, they asked, "What could we do more, better or differently to continue improving our level of customer service, thus increasing our approval rating?" Each meeting provided ideas for improvement, some big and some small. When they were implemented, all of these ideas contributed to a customer service rating of 93% in eighteen months! While that represented on average less than two percent improvement each month, the continuous process of asking the right questions inspired everyone to keep going until they had the second best ratings in their Fortune 500 company. They also reduced customer "hold time" from 20 minutes to under 20 seconds.

Individual and group commitment to an effective action plan is the purpose of the entire Framework process. The results achieved depend on the quality of the plan and the degree of ownership, or commitment, to implementing it. As individual team members get highly involved in the solution steps, the process reaffirms their commitment to results. They are naturally going to be highly committed to the ideas they have contributed. A way to frame that is:

Results = Quality of Plan x Degree of Buy-in

A great plan with poor buy-in yields poor results. A mediocre plan with high buy-in yields good results. When the Framework for Leadership is used, the plan improves significantly due to the benefits that are derived from the Forward Focus perspective. People work harder and smarter to create a quality plan and their ownership builds in the process. The results are excellent, and often extraordinary.

Accountability

There is a second part of Step 5 that is critically important. The responses to this question determine who will be responsible for specific tasks. It is imperative that everyone be clear about their specific role and the expectations established for that role. The basic question is:

Who will do what by when?

For about a year after developing the basic Framework for Leadership, we didn't have an accountability question.

As a result, we generated good plans, but implementation sometimes suffered. Plans aren't useful unless someone is accountable for implementing them.

We remember the first time we used this accountability question, "Who will do what by when?" in our own company's strategic planning process. We were curious to see people's responses, because now we were asking them to take responsibility for action. Would they really want to do the work? They enjoyed the creative process, but would they actually sign up for the activities required to accomplish the results we wanted? As it turned out, any questions or concerns we might have had were unjustified. We learned that when people are creatively involved in planning the solutions, they are eager to participate in the implementation! People volunteered to do things we didn't even know they could do.

Do people have "glass ceilings?" You bet! However, asking "Who is willing or would like to do this?" can remove, or at least raise, those ceilings in our minds as people step up to the need. They aren't likely to volunteer for things for which they have no capacity.

Ed's older daughter, Robin, was a college student who managed to squeeze four years of college into five years.☺ Yes, she approved this comment. So, when Robin came to work at Enlightened Leadership while she "looked for a real job," Ed wasn't expecting her to contribute a great deal. Imagine his proud surprise when Robin was quick to respond with an enthusiastic, "I'll do that!" when the team was asked "Who will do what by when?"

Caution: The initial action plan does not need to fully accomplish the objective. Because the ultimate goal is likely to be large or complex, you should not demand that a comprehensive plan evolve overnight. There is little value in putting undue pressure on yourself and your team to develop all the answers at once. The initial plan might simply involve some research, discussing the scope with stakeholders, or experimenting with a specific approach. Too much pressure could actually stifle the creative process – and it is a *process*. Remember, it's far more important to generate an interim action plan that gets you moving *toward* a solution.

Step 5 is the *beginning* of the action plan. You will have plenty of opportunities to fill in more of the pieces that contribute to the final solution as you move along.

The Solution Might Come Quickly

On the other hand, be open to the possibility of "miracle" solutions …brilliant ideas that are easy to implement and achieve major results very quickly.

Penny's Disease Control Team, mentioned in Chapter 1, quickly developed the breakthrough ideas about how to provide lower costs while maintaining isolated housing for tuberculosis patients. This happened almost immediately after the team shifted from a problem-orientation to a solution-orientation. That shift happened easily and early in the five-step Framework process. Those initial solutions continue to save the county approximately $250,000 every quarter while providing a higher quality of living for the patients.

Measuring Progress

There is one more important aspect of Step 5. Now is the time to determine how progress will be evaluated. While you could establish measurement criteria in the goal-setting of Step 3, it would tend to limit your options for solutions. By waiting until you have brainstormed ways to reach your objective before establishing measurement criteria, your team is allowed to think outside the box about solutions. Once solution ideas are in hand, deciding how to measure progress forces additional clarity about the goal. The basic question is:

How will we measure progress?

It Does Not Take Experts to Facilitate

When A. J. Hiltenbrand, mentioned in chapter 1, facilitated the Finding Profits Workshop for dozens of people from several European countries, his role was to provide some context for the work, teach the forty-some people how to utilize the Framework process, and then step back and watch them do it. While he was available for support, the primary facilitation was actually done by the participants who were divided into logical, functional groups of four to six people. Some parts of the facilitation went more smoothly than others, yet they all produced substantial results.

You don't have to be a trained facilitator to use this tool. In fact, so many cost savings and additional profits were uncovered in that one meeting that the participants immediately committed to holding another session the following year for four more European countries.

When we ask the Step 5 Effective Questions, the value of the Framework for Leadership comes together as the Action Plan is established and the assigned responsibilities for the solution are determined. The basic questions are:

What can we do more, better or differently to move closer to our objective?
and ***Who will do what by when?***
and ***How will we measure progress?***

All five steps of the Framework for Leadership have been presented. The next chapter brings all five steps together and looks at the entire process.

Questions to Think About:

How clear is the action plan by those who have to implement it on a project with which you are involved?

How clear is the acountability on the critical path to success?

How well do established measures identify the real progress of the project?

Pulling It All Together

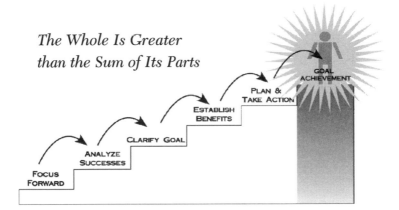

*The Whole Is Greater
than the Sum of Its Parts*

We are now ready to put together all five steps of the Framework for Leadership.

Step 1. What is already working?

Step 2. What makes it work?

Step 3. What are we trying to accomplish?

Step 4. What are the benefits of achieving the objective?

*Step 5. What can we do more, better or differently
to move closer to the objective?*

Let's review all five steps to see how they fit together. We start by asking:

1. "What is already working? What successes have we had? What is working well? What are you pleased about?"

   These types of questions are very useful for priming the pump of creativity and becoming solution focused. The responses develop positive energy and enthusiasm. Because the questions focus on what is working, they tend to be safe to answer. This builds trust. When energy is high and trust is strong, creative problem-solving is unleashed.

The second step is:

2. "What makes it work? What caused that success? To what do you attribute that success? What about this success pleases you the most? What specific talents most contributed to the success?"

These are questions that organizations and people seldom ask, yet the costs of not asking them are substantial. When a team really understands the cause of a success, they can leverage that knowledge in other situations. Organizations tend to be quick to perform root-cause analysis of problems, yet they seldom do root-cause analysis of successes.

Asking "What makes it work?" is energizing, because it invites the acknowledgement of specific people as they are describing what they contributed to the success.

The next question is:

3. "What is the objective? or What are we trying to accomplish?"

Having built participation, acknowledgement and learning in the first two steps, this third step is an opportunity to look at the objectives to determine if they're the right ones, and to see if everyone is on the same track. When the team members are involved in determining the objectives, they are more likely accountable for achieving it.

Having established the objective, the next step is:

4. "What are the benefits of accomplishing it? What will it do for each of the stakeholders?"

This is the buy-in step. When people are clear about what's in it for them, you can stand back and watch things get done. If they aren't clear about the personal benefits, good luck getting anything done, no matter what you do. This step is particularly important when launching a major project or initiating a turnaround or change situation, where substantial buy-in is needed from the start.

The fifth step is:

5. "What can we do more, better or differently to move closer to the objective?" "Who will do what by when?" "How will we measure progress?"

These questions take advantage of the creativity that's been built, and the clarity of the goal that's been established to determine the action plan and the individual tasks and the accountability for those tasks. The power in this step comes from the creative energy generated in the other steps. Again, you allow the complete action plan to naturally evolve over time.

Where Does the Problem Show-up?

Let's pause to ask a question about this process. Are we ignoring the problem? If not, where does the "problem" show up in the Framework?

You probably realized the "problem" is merely the gap between Step 1, "What is already working?" and Step 3, "What are we trying to accomplish?" To solve the "problem," just do what's necessary to close the gap.

No one wants to be part of the problem, but everyone wants to be part of the solution.

Imagine starting a meeting by throwing the problem onto the conference room table. Can you sense people posturing to make sure they don't get blamed for the problem? Now imagine using the entirely different approach of clarifying where you already are (What's working?), looking at where you want to go (What do we want to accomplish?), and realizing the challenge is to close the gap between the two. The first approach creates defensiveness, and the second approach shifts people to a solution-orientation.

No one wants to be part of the problem, but *everyone* wants to be part of the solution.

Circle of Transformation™

By using the Framework for Leadership as a continuous process, the possibility of breakthrough ideas, or transformation, is enhanced. Since Step 5 is the action plan, the next step would be the implementation. Once the plan is being implemented, it is important to monitor and communicate progress continually.

To do that, start with Step 1 again, "What is working so far?" Celebrating the early successes opens creativity for the next steps and keeps the focus on the next level of solution. Analyzing those successes in Step 2, "What is causing those successes?" adds more enthusiasm and creativity to the process. Checking in on Step 3, "What are we trying to accomplish?" might determine the goal has not changed.

However, as this circular process continues through multiple cycles, there may be a time when a realization occurs that the "real" goal is something else. When that happens, the new clarity is virtually always inspiring. In *The Leadership Engine,* Noel Tichy said, "Winning organizations not only fulfill their desired goals today, but they also continually redesign those goals as circumstances change, and go on to meet those new goals."[14] If the goal has not changed, there might be little need to review Step 4, "What are the benefits for all the stakeholders?" Step 5 is nearly always critical, "What else can we do to move closer to the goal?"

The following graphic illustrates the circular nature of the Framework for Leadership in practice. In this continuous improvement version, it is called the Circle of Transformation.

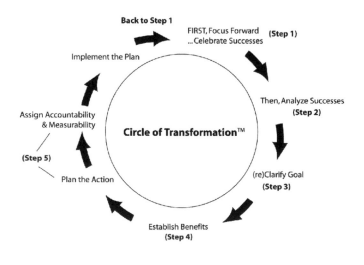

Specific Applications

There are many different applications for the Framework for Leadership. Examples include:

- Conflict resolution
- Win-win negotiation
- Team & individual performance improvement
- Forward Focused project reviews
- Problem-solving
- Developing collaboration and teamwork
- Effective project startup
- Effective selling

As the Framework is used for different applications, the questions likely need to be adapted to better fit the context. Each of the examples on the following pages introduces possible modifications of the Framework for Leadership questions for a particular application.

Framework for Personal Conflict Resolution:

1. What are some things you appreciate about each other? ...what else?
2. What, specifically, do you appreciate about that?
3. What is your common goal or interest in this situation?
4. What would be the benefit for each of you to accomplish that?
5. What could each of you do to move closer to that goal? ...what else?

To use the Framework in different situations, simply modify the generic questions to fit the specific need. For example, in a personal conflict resolution situation, the first question, "What is already working?" doesn't make sense. Instead, change it to something like, "What are some things you appreciate about each other?" The important element is that the question generates positive, Forward Focused answers.

It is always valuable to ask "What else?" a number of times to more fully develop the substance and energy of the responses.

Framework for Win-Win Negotiation:

1. Where do we already agree? Where else?
2. What is it about those situations that cause us to agree?
3. What are the overall goals that are important to us?
4. How will we benefit from accomplishing those goals?
5. What one thing could either of us do right now to move closer to those goals? …what else?

The first step establishes the context of the entire process. In this case, building on the agreements rather than dwelling on differences.

Framework for
Individual Performance Improvement:

1. What are the areas of your performance about which you feel best? What are some of your successes? ...what else?

2. What personal strengths specifically support those successes? What else?

3. What are the most important objectives of your role?

4. What would be the benefits to the team when you accomplish those? To you personally?

5. What are some specific things you can do to come closer to meeting those objectives? ...what else? What help do you need?

Think about the value of having frequent one-on-one meetings with each of your team members to have these discussions. By doing so, continuous improvement is a real possibility, and there will be no surprises when the "annual performance review" takes place.

Also, it is exactly these types of questions which we want the employee to be continually asking herself.

Framework for
Forward Focused Project Reviews:

1. What successes have we had since our last project review?

2. What specifically caused those successes? What can we learn from them?

3. What specific objectives are each of us working on right now?

4. What are the benefits to the overall project by accomplishing those? What are the benefits to your team? What will it do for you personally?

5. What specific actions can you take now to move closer to your objectives? Who will be responsible for those actions, and when will you complete them?

Notice how this approach keeps everyone Forward Focused and solution-oriented.

Framework for Problem Resolution:

1. Although we do have this significant challenge, what are some things that are working, no matter how small? What else?
2. To what do we attribute those successes?
3. What is the specific goal we are trying to achieve in this situation?
4. What would be the benefits of accomplishing that objective (for all stakeholders)?
5. What could we do more, better or differently to move past this challenge and closer to our objective? Who will do what by when?

The key to problem resolution is to avoid the blame game, and build energy for finding solutions by focusing first on successes and what is working – rather than the traditional "analyze the problem." Remember, the problem is only the gap between where you are, from a positive perspective, and where you want to be (the objective). With that Forward Focused perspective of the "problem," our experience reveals that people will be eager to contribute to the solution.

Framework for
Developing Collaboration and Teamwork:

1. What are some things we are doing well to work together as a team? What else? What are some things that worked well on other teams of which you have been a part?

2. What, specifically, caused each of those to work?

3. What is our vision of excellent collaboration and teamwork? What else?

4. What would be the benefits for each of the parties involved to accomplish that vision?

5. What can we do to move closer to that vision? What is each of us willing and committed to contribute?

This approach creates a vision of ideal collaboration and teamwork, thus giving the team clarity and focus on where they want to be and how to get there instead of staying stuck in the problems they are currently having.

Framework for Effective Project Startup:

1. What have you done successfully in similar projects?
2. What did you do as a project team that made it so successful? What else?
3. What is your vision of how we want to work together on this project?
4. What are the benefits of doing so? For your clients, stakeholders, company, ourselves?
5. What are some things we could do:
   a. To move forward in those ways?
   b. To keep on track?
   c. To get back on track when we waver?
   d. What commitment will each project team member make toward contributing to this vision?

Rather than waiting until we have problems on the project team, with this approach, we are deciding at the beginning how we want to work together. We are building a model based on our diverse experiences on other project teams.

Framework for Effective Selling:

1. What do you like about your current service (product)? What else?

2. What is the specific advantage of each of those to you?

3. If you could describe the ideal service (product), what would it be? What else? How would (your differentiating feature) fit into your ideal?

4. What would be the benefits (to all stakeholders) to have the ideal service (product), or close to it? What would be the perceived value?

5. Step 5 in this case is not a question. Instead, it is your proposal for how you could support filling the gap between what they currently have and their ideal. If you cannot meet what they currently like and also fill the gap, or at least come close, you might not have a good solution.

This is a powerful approach to selling which builds trust by focusing on what is already working. You are not directly asking them to share the problems they have that might be sensitive. The problems *will* come out, because you develop the gap between what is already working and what they would ideally like to have. Because of the trust built, they will likely go into great detail about their problems later in the process – when it is easier for you to be more direct.

Summary

A number of applications have been presented using all five steps of the Framework, and suggested modifications have been made for each of the different contexts. The next chapter will provide a shortened version of the Framework that is often useful.

Questions to Think About:

What is a specific situation for which you could use the essence of the Framework to develop a solution?

What is the first step question that you would ask for that context?

9

Sometimes It Can Be Even Simpler!

I t's easy to argue that the five-step Framework for Leadership is a simple approach to deal collaboratively with your greatest management challenges, yet often it can be even simpler. You don't always need all five steps. Several examples follow:

The "mini" Framework

Ed wanted those people reporting to him to evaluate his performance, so he called a meeting, and invited them to answer two questions. The first was a typical, positive, or Forward Focused question such as, "What do you appreciate about how I work with you?" or, "What am I doing well in my role?"

Traditionally, the next question would be the challenging one – the "What's wrong?" question, or "What needs improvement?" or "What do you see as my issue?" or

"What do I do poorly?" No matter how it's worded, the follow-up question tends to be seen as problematic. It often causes defensiveness. In the best case, the question might be phrased as, "Where do I need improvement?"

As you might imagine, however, Ed's second question was a little different ... "What would you like to see me do even better than I'm already doing?" Think about that question. What is the implication? Well, it implies that Ed was already doing well *to some degree* in most everything he was doing – which was true. (And it's true for everyone). Notice that there is nothing to get defensive about. Everyone can always do *even* better, whatever his current level of performance. In our experience, there is something magical in the "even better" terminology.

To summarize this simple performance appraisal process, Ed posed two questions:

1. From your perspective, what am I already doing well in my role?
2. What would you like to see me do even better?

The first time Ed facilitated this process, he was overwhelmed with the value and quality of the feedback he received. With that second question, there were no "need to's" or "should's" about Ed's performance. There was no sense of judgment, only comments such as, "I would like to see you acknowledge me when I do good work more often than you already do." How could you get defensive over that type of feedback? Notice how the quality of the response is directly related to the quality of the question.

Because of the way the feedback was given, Ed could really hear it, and the people felt listened to. It was such an open and powerful experience for Ed that he has encouraged managers from all over the world to try it for themselves. The key to the success of the process was that both questions were Forward Focused. There was no "What's wrong?" oriented question to create defensiveness.

The generic mini Framework often looks like:

1. **What are we already doing well?**
2. **What could we do even better?**

Notice that this simply consists of Steps 1 and 5 of the Framework for Leadership.

It's Your Ship

In his excellent and bestselling book, *It's Your Ship: Management Techniques From the Best Damn Ship in the Navy*, Commander Mike Abrashoff reported using his own version of a mini Framework when he asked each sailor on his crew of the U.S.S. Benfold the following three questions: [15]

1. What do you like most about your experience on the U.S.S. Benfold?
2. What do you like least about your experience on the Benfold?
3. What would you change if you could?

All three questions are Forward Focused, including the second one. Think about it. Note the difference between "What do you like least?" vs. "What do you NOT like?" What do you think would have happened if the sailors on board the Benfold had been asked, "What don't you like about your experience on the Benfold?" Responses would probably have been something like, "Nothing, sir! I like everything, sir!" But truthfully, everyone has *something* that he likes the "least." So the question is not threatening when worded as "What do you like least?" This is an example of a subtle change that makes a profound difference. As a result, Commander Abrashoff got honest, useful answers.

By the time the interviews were finished, he knew exactly what was working well on the Benfold and what needed attention. The interview process had a great impact on his priorities for turning around the poorly performing ship and dramatically improving morale. Three of the many impressive results included: 1) becoming the top performing ship in the history of the Pacific fleet; 2) retaining 100% of its crew; 3) returning nearly 20% of its budget to Navy coffers.

Let's be clear. Mike Abrashoff had not read our book, nor had he participated in any of our workshops. His own quest to be a more effective leader led him to discover these simple tools for himself.

When Time is Limited ...

Many opportunities arise during the day that could incorporate the essence of the Framework by helping people feel acknowledged and getting them focused on what's important. Think of all those hallway or water cooler conversations that might utilize simple Step 1 and 5 questions like:

What are you feeling good about? What successes are you having? What else?

What, specifically, are you looking to improve over the next couple of weeks? What ideas do you have for doing that?

A conversation premised on these simple questions could last just a couple of minutes, or it could lead to additional discussions, if appropriate. Either way, there is an opportunity to provide value by asking the right questions.

A Great Golf Instructor

Ed's golf instructor, Bud Bellis, uses the essence of the Framework for Leadership all the time in his instruction, and he has certainly never heard of the Framework. It is just what he discovered is the most effective way of teaching. In a typical lesson, Bud watches the student hit some balls, and he finds something to acknowledge or praise, even if it is minor. He repeats this for nearly every swing. That is Step 1 of the Framework. He rarely tells them what they are doing wrong, because he does not want them focusing on that.

Next, Bud tells the student something specific he wants them to do. Here he is creating an objective or goal, which is Step 3 of the Framework. For example, he might say, "I want you to pretend that the golf ball is six inches in front of where it really is. Your job is to hit all the way through that imaginary ball before coming up." The student then acts on his instruction, and Bud goes back to telling him what he is doing well. He lets the student practice this new objective until he is ready to provide a different objective. All along, Bud is simply acknowledging what the student is doing well and providing him with the next-step instruction for what he needs to do so he can be even better. And those next steps are always simple! Bud calls his teaching method "tweaking."

Bud does sometimes talk about what the student is doing wrong, but those comments are few compared to the praise he provides. He is naturally teaching from the essence of the Framework, and we believe that is the key to making him a great instructor. When Ed shared this story with his instructor, Bud said simply, "You pretty much nailed my approach!"

Audits Made Fun!

Audits are an application that could utilize the "mini" Framework. If someone walked into your office and said, "The auditors are coming tomorrow morning," what would you think or feel?

The auditing group of a mid-sized CPA firm in Minneapolis knew that their clients were seldom happy to see them. After experiencing the EQ process of the Framework, they immediately saw the possibility of changing the negative image of auditors and the auditing process.

One of them said, "Wow. It sure would be different if our clients felt that our intention was to document and share all the ways they were *already* being effective and how they could be even better. They would look forward to our audits!"

"That might be a bit exaggerated," laughed another CPA, "but it sure would make the whole process a more positive experience for them… and us, too." They left the session committed to changing the relationship with their auditing clients.

Imagine if all auditors shifted to this "What is working?" and "What could work even better?" mindset with the idea to do a "successful practice" audit! Perhaps you really would look forward to the arrival of the auditors!

When You Are Clear about Objectives and Benefits...

Here is another time to simplify the Framework process. When you're in the middle of a project and you're clear about its objectives and the benefits, you don't need to review them every time you meet. Periodically, there might be value in verifying that the goals haven't changed, but not every time.

For example, if you had a meeting last week that resulted in a very clear objective for your team's project, you can skip Step 3, "What is our objective?" when you have your next project review.

Utilizing the Effective Question process of the Framework to promote continuous improvement, you often only need to ask:

1. **What is already working?**
2. **What could we/you do even better?**

While these questions are usually quite powerful, there are certain situations that can arise in which a completely Forward Focused approach might not work. Learn how to deal with that special case in the next chapter.

10

Emotions in the Workplace: Dealing with Reality

There is a time when Forward Focus and Effective Questions do not work to shift negative mindsets.

You have likely experienced such situations possibly where you were discussing an idea, project or a change for which you wanted buy-in and commitment. Perhaps everyone was quiet, or some were nodding their heads in agreement, but the sense of commitment was not there. Something was missing or was not being discussed. The proverbial elephant or skunk was in the room. Some knew what it was, but no one was talking. You could only feel the fear and concern that was limiting people's ability to focus forward in any way.

The idea of Forward Focus won't work when someone is afraid or so stuck in negative emotions that they can't shift. The best way to deal with those concerns is to put them on the table so they can be discussed and defused. A simple way of doing that is by asking:

What concerns do you have?

The Ultimate BACKWARD Focus

Fear is the ultimate *backward* focus. It paralyzes us, because we are so focused on thinking of the worst that could happen that we are prevented from consciously choosing to focus forward.

Years ago, when Don Lamb was a captain in the Colorado State Patrol, he was trying to have an important discussion with his team, but they were holding back. After some time in this restrained mode, Don said, "I need to ask all of you a question. What are you fearing right now?" After a few moments of total silence, someone opened up about their concerns. Others soon followed and they had a great discussion, because people were able to surface their fears and concerns. That allowed the group to reach the depth the important topic deserved.

Another example of a team holding back because of concerns occurred on a recent trek on Mount Kilimanjaro in East Africa. Our team was quieter than usual while having pre-dinner tea at the 15,000-foot summit base camp. Ralph Johnson, our Swedish friend, was particularly quiet, which was unlike him under normal conditions. Ed felt that any attempted discussion would be superficial unless the hidden issue was uncovered and diffused.

Ed asked Ralph if it was okay to ask him a direct question. Getting his permission, he asked, "What concerns do you have about what happened on the trail today?" Although silent until then, Ralph quickly indicated that some feelings might have been hurt when some of us broke away from the slower group to reach camp sooner. Five or six people then contributed to a great conversation about the situation, sharing different perspectives. That got the team past the concerns, and allowed us to refocus on the major challenge of climbing the mountain. It was a critical moment for our team. Ralph expressed appreciation for the question, and acknowledged the value of the team discussion.

Miraculous Facilitation

At the time of the following experience that demonstrated both the debilitating effects of negative emotions and a way to deal with them, Carol Bergmann, consultant and author of *Managing Your Energy at Work*, [16] was a regional quality manager for a large professional software services firm. She was often called in to support different management teams and groups across the country. This situation occurred in their Austin office where a group of people was providing help desk service for a key client. They were having major issues and the relationship with the client was strained.

Carol investigated and found that the management team had done a good job of meeting with employees and listening to the issues, yet they couldn't come up with a solution. So, Carol, who had just been introduced to the Framework by Doug Krug, decided to give it a try.

She walked into the meeting room, and reports she could have cut the negative atmosphere with a knife! It was horrible – very tense. Given this environment, Carol made an excellent decision. She decided she could *not* start this meeting with "What is working?" First, she felt she needed to let them vent their hostilities. So, she asked instead, "What is the situation you're dealing with? What's going on?" (That was her way of saying, "What concerns do you have?") After that opening, Carol was flooded with all their issues. This process dissipated their negative energy and fears, which was exactly what Carol wanted. Only then were they prepared to look at the possibility of being Forward Focused.

So, with that preparation, Carol took a deep breath and asked, "I've heard a lot of the problems. What's *working* on this project? Since you've been at it for a year and a half, something must be working." There was dead silence, and Carol allowed that silence as she waited patiently – an often important aspect of facilitation. After what seemed like an eternity, one woman mentioned a report that she had created for the group that was helpful to their communications. With a little less silence this time, another woman mentioned a tool that she had developed that had been helpful to the team and the client. Then the successes came more and more rapidly. Carol filled five flip charts with their successes on the project, and for each of those, she drilled deeper to capture the cause of the success or a better understanding of it (Step 2). The positive energy was amazing! The entire atmosphere had completely, and dramatically, turned around.

Sometimes, the most Effective Question you can ask is a question that allows people to share their concerns, their fears, or whatever is keeping them stuck – before inviting them to Focus Forward again.

From there, Carol moved to Step 3, "What are you trying to accomplish?" She specifically needed to know what they *wanted* to accomplish and what they felt they *could* accomplish, given the limitations they were facing. They established their goals clearly and positively, and then discussed the benefits of accomplishing them. The energy remained high and positive, and even increased during the benefits discussion.

When they were ready for Step 5, the Action Plan, Carol got out of the way and let the staff do the work. The enthusiasm with which they created their plans was impressive. They realized that they had their own solutions all along, but had been waiting for management to solve their problems and tell them what to do. That break-through was a miracle! The only thing they really needed from management was a pizza budget.

Two months later Carol visited the group to see how they were doing. They were well along on implementing their plans; they were meeting frequently over pizza, and using the Framework to continue the process they had started. Most importantly, the project was back on track and the relationship with the client had been mended in a major way.

Sometimes, the most Effective Question you can ask is a question that allows people to share their concerns, their fears, or whatever is keeping them stuck – before inviting them to Focus Forward again. It might look like:

- What concerns do you have about this situation?
- What's not being said?
- What's going on?
- What am I missing in this discussion?
- What fears do you have about this?
- What is the "elephant" in the room that is not being discussed?

The next chapter provides a number of true stories of how the Framework was applied in different situations. It will show the flexibility of the process.

A Question to Think About:

What highly charged challenge that you face might benefit from inviting people to address concerns up front – then shifting toward solution?

11

Learn From Real Examples!

The 5-step process in the Framework for Leadership is adaptable and flexible for use in various real-world situations. The example topics covered in this chapter include:

- Planning and Implementation
- Managing Cross-functional Project Teams
- Gaining Buy-In for Change
- Creating Collaboration in a Difficult Situation
- Creating Visions or Ideal Models
- Conflict Resolution
- Running Forums with Multiple Stakeholders

Planning and Implementation

After being introduced to the Framework, Tony Lynn, the founder and owner of a mid-sized leather importer based in North Carolina, invited team members to his house one Saturday. His intent was to use the process to do some joint planning for the new year.

Since he'd never taken this particular approach, he wasn't sure what would happen, but he courageously launched into the process. Right away, people started sharing successes. Enthusiasm grew. While it was very positive and energizing for the group, there were no real surprises until he reached Step 3, "What objectives do you want to have for next year that would really motivate you?"

Tony was surprised when the team established some lofty goals – ones he wasn't sure they could accomplish. One goal seemed especially impossible: moving out of their warehouse and office (that had another two years on the existing lease) into a better, larger space. Tony didn't think such an envisioned space even existed in the area. He certainly didn't think moving was possible – given the lease situation.

Immediately after this goal-clarifying meeting, Tony's team began to work diligently on the projects and used the Framework EQs for review and to keep the team progressing. They stayed focused and enthusiastic as they experienced success after success – energized further by celebrating each of them. All of this occurred with very little help from Tony, who was traveling extensively.

He was ecstatic, therefore, when the team accomplished several annual goals within six months, including moving into a beautiful new office and warehouse space. They had done the seemingly impossible. The ideas and enthusiasm generated in that meeting at Tony's house had begun a positive spiral of actions leading to results.

Furthermore, Tony felt the Framework process was easy to use in the collaborative planning phase, and the team used it effectively in the implementation phase.

Managing Cross-functional Project Teams

In another example, Rancho Cordova had sought to become its own city a couple of times without success. With vision and a focus on the future, the Board of Directors of the Rancho Cordova Chamber of Commerce engaged its members and energized the community for another try. Lee Casaleggio was asked to facilitate the Board's two year planning meeting that preceded the incorporation election. In a fairly conventional but energetic 2-day retreat, the Board worked long hours to create the blueprint of activities and accountabilities needed for success.

Six months later, after Lee, an outstanding facilitator, had been through an Enlightened Leadership Train-the-Facilitator course, he met with the Board again. They convened to assess progress on the plan, which had some significant issues. Lee proposed that they use the Framework for Leadership, explaining that it was a different way of approaching this type of meeting. Reaction was immediate:

"Aren't we going to discuss the problems we're having?"

"No," Lee said.

"What!!?" was the incredulous reply.

Lee asked for their trust and received a grudging go-ahead.

With the first question: "In implementing our plan, where have we been successful?" examples exploded from members. Members interrupted each other to share achievements. They had entries on 16 separate chart pads hung around the room.

With the second question: "What has caused these successes?" the group turned quietly analytical, but not for long. The energy behind the flow of cause and effect responses mirrored the success stories. As they filled the chart pads, a trend appeared: the name of the Chamber's Executive Director appeared as a primary cause for success on 14 of the sheets.

"I get it!" came the cry from the member who had asked if they were going to discuss problems. She went on: "In all our previous meetings we used the time to beat up on our Director for all the things that had not gotten done. Clearly, what we see on our walls is that we've spread the Director too thin. We've got to get more of us involved."

At this point, Lee is fond of recalling that there was a tear on the Director's cheek. The need for more help had always been there. It was simply invisible from the focus on problems.

Questions 3 and 4 were swiftly and joyfully completed – the group was committed to incorporation, and was both passionate and clear about the benefits to every level of the community.

The Step 5 question: "What do we need to do more, better or differently?" was answered by rapid volunteering for support assignments and delegation of tasks. The Framework for Leadership became a framework for *success* with the citizens' vote of approval on November 5, 2002 and incorporation of the City of Rancho Cordova on July 1, 2003.

Getting Buy-In for a Change

A division of a major pharmaceutical company was making a change in compensation for its manufacturing workers. Sharon, a key department manager, knew this could be a very big challenge. Having been introduced to the Framework shortly before, she decided to facilitate a discussion about the new compensation plan. She didn't know of a better approach, so the risk didn't seem too high.

Using the Framework, she asked people to examine which aspects of the new compensation program they liked. Then she asked what they specifically liked about those aspects. She asked plenty of "What else?" questions and then reviewed the new plan's objectives, which were set by corporate. Next, she facilitated a discussion about the benefits of achieving those objectives – for the customer, the company, the division, the team and for each of them individually.

Finally, Sharon asked the employees to look at how the plan met the objectives and even invited them to propose ways to make it better – with the proviso that she didn't have the last word on those decisions.

By the end of the process, Sharon was delighted to find that she'd achieved a good level of buy-in for the new plan, which had rarely happened in the past. Employee skepticism was minimal, and they acknowledged her for having facilitated an open discussion about the compensation plan. She credited the Forward Focused approach of the Framework for the success. The workers also came up with a few ideas for improving the system, some of which Sharon was able to implement.

Creating Collaboration in a Difficult Situation

The Chamber of Commerce of a major western city was about to conduct its annual off-site meeting of the volunteer Board of Directors and the permanent staff members. The new president and staff were nervous about the meeting because they had just fired their president after 16 years of service. There were concerns about the impact of this change on the meeting since half the people thought firing the president was the best thing they could have done, and the other half thought it was the worst thing.

Ed was asked to facilitate the meeting of approximately 40 people. The objective of the multi-day event was to develop a model for how the volunteer Board and permanent staff could work most effectively together. This was a contentious topic due to some recent issues between the Board and the staff.

Ed was unsure how this meeting would go, or even how to lead the facilitation, so he did what he had learned to trust. After setting the context for the conference, and providing some background about the Framework for Leadership, he began with Step 1 by asking the group, "What are examples of past successes in which the Board and staff have worked well together?"

As they responded, Ed then asked, "What specifically was it about how the Board and staff worked together to create that particular success? (Step 2) They filled several easel charts with successes and several more with their corresponding reasons. Although these were very encouraging, Ed didn't quite know what to do with them.

He moved to the third question of the Framework and almost held his breath as he asked, "How would you describe the ideal model of how the Board and staff could work together most effectively?" He was not at all clear about what they might say – or even if they'd say anything.

His concerns were unjustified. Instantly one of the younger board members, Jeff Julin, President of MGA Communications, raised his hand. "You've already got the model, Ed, it's those three charts. It's all those things that we've done in the past to work together to create those successes. That's our ideal model of how to work together most effectively."

"Thank you, Jeff!" Ed was pleased that the model had evolved so easily, though he had been unable to see in advance how it was going to occur. Once again, Ed had reason to trust the process of the Framework.

To make sure the model was complete, Ed also asked, "What else would you add to make the model even more complete?" Several excellent ideas were contributed to enhance the model, and the energy level in the room was electrifying.

The "What would be the benefits of effectively implementing this model?" question generated high buy-in and even more energy because there were so many benefits for all the stakeholders. That positive synergy was then used over the remaining days of the conference to look at specific actions they could take to implement the new model in practical ways and real-world situations.

Years later, people involved in that meeting still recall how it proved to be a turning point for the Chamber.

Creating Visions or Ideal Models

One of the Framework's greatest strengths is developing collaborative visions or ideal models. The third step, "What are we trying to accomplish?" becomes "What is our ideal model or vision of what we want to do?"

Now, we want to warn you. Sometimes, we take our work home with us. This process can be rewarding even in very personal relationships. Such an example occurred between Ed and Jonette when they were first engaged. They wanted to create their ideal relationship vision. Since they knew the Framework was just the ticket for doing this, they planned an entire evening at a quiet, romantic restaurant. They brought pads of paper and pens to use.

After ordering dinner, they began with "What do we already appreciate about each other or our relationship?" They took turns sharing, and of course, kept asking, "What else?" When something shared was more of a surface factor, they would ask the other person to go deeper with precisely what they appreciated and why (Step 2). Jonette and Ed filled up several sheets with responses from the first two steps. It was a great way to spend an evening (in mutual admiration), so they were in no hurry to finish.

When they had exhausted ideas for Steps 1 and 2, they moved on to the final step – in this particular process – Step 3, "What is our ideal relationship vision?" As soon as they asked that question, they realized they already knew! Most of it was everything they already appreciated about their relationship. They just needed to simplify the vision using all of their notes.

Furthermore, this was an important opportunity to look at aspects of their ideal vision that might not currently be strong in their relationship. This was the most challenging part, as this represented gaps and even issues in their current relationship. The deep sharing of appreciation in the first two steps, though, had opened their hearts and prepared them for a new level of openness and honesty. The process moved smoothly and lovingly and supported some deep, heartfelt discussion.

The resulting "Jonette and Ed's Relationship Vision" was calligraphied, framed and hung in their bedroom. Every now and then, it serves as a tool to remind them of their shared vision! The process was powerful, and the symbol of that process, the framed piece, continues to be an important reminder of their sacred relationship.

Conflict Resolution

Susan Dixon, an assistant principal attending one of Doug's workshops, reported that she needed to deal with a sensitive situation that afternoon involving two co-teachers. Although the two had been good friends, the relationship had deteriorated and was beginning to impact the quality of their teaching with even parents showing concern.

She had scheduled a meeting with the quarreling teachers for that afternoon. Having been introduced to the Framework in the morning, she thought it might have a chance of working – at least better than any other ideas she had!

Susan set the context for the meeting by sharing that she had some reasons to be concerned about the teachers' relationship and how it was affecting the students. She suggested that she wanted to facilitate a specific discussion. After reminding the teachers that they had been good friends, she jumped into the process by asking, "What are some of the things each of you appreciates about the other?"

There was a long silence before one teacher acknowledged the other for something she appreciated. The other teacher was then motivated to share something good about her co-teacher. A series of "what else?" questions was key here. As they loosened up, the comments and responses got stronger and deeper as they gradually shifted their mindset back to what they really appreciated about each other. Occasionally, Susan would say, "Say more about that" or something similar to encourage depth and sincerity.

By this time, the statements were quite positive and elevated. The co-workers were remembering what they had appreciated about each other all along. Because of a recent conflict, which did not need to be discussed at all, they had been distracted and had lost focus of the more important aspects of their relationship.

Now that they were back on track, Susan asked, "What is your common goal here?" (Step 3) It only took a split second for both of them to jump in and confirm that it was, indeed, to provide the best possible education for their students.

"Well, it's certainly clear to me that you have the right goal," Susan said. "What are some things each of you can do to make sure you're accomplishing that goal?" As they responded to this question, there was a whole different level of energy, enthusiasm and focus. They were back in a friendly relationship and moving forward together again.

Back in Doug's session the next day, Susan reported that the last she saw of them, they were walking arm in arm down the hallway energetically discussing plans to promote a great learning environment in their classroom.

Running Forums with Multiple Stakeholders

Cathy Singletary, a division manager in a major Social Services agency's Children's Services Division, uses the Framework in many different ways – training, best known practices, quality assurance, legislative implementation, development of policy & procedure, etc. The application she likes best has to do with the Community Forums where she goes to the community for their input on the Child Welfare Strategic Plan.

When the forums were just beginning, Cathy's director wouldn't let her use the Framework for Leadership in the community groups because he felt it was too risky. The meetings were full of dissension and disagreement. The Director then gave the go ahead because "It couldn't be any worse than what they already tried!" Use of the 5 steps of the Framework was overwhelmingly successful and resulted in a strategic plan with strong community buy-in – they felt heard and became a part of the solution. Now, it's just the way they do business. What evolved was the acceptance of the Framework as a continual quality improvement tool.

These examples represent just a few applications of the Framework. What are some specific issues or situations you face where the Framework could be useful? Use the space on the next page to make some notes for yourself.

_____

_____

_____

_____

_____

_____

_____

_____

_____

Questions to Think About:

What application ideas do you have for the Framework for Leadership?

What is one area that could provide the most leverage for your effort?

12

The Questions Work and It's Not Really about the Questions

"The scarcest resource in the world today is leadership talent capable of continuously transforming organizations to win in tomorrow's world."[17]

Noel Tichy, professor,
University of Michigan Business School
Author, *The Leadership Engine*

We've provided eight questions that the best leaders ask consistently and frequently. These questions can be transformational for your situations, the people you influence and yourself. Let's review the generic versions:

1.   What is already working?

2.   What makes it work?

3.   What are we trying to accomplish?

4.   What would be the benefits of achieving those objectives?

5, 6. & 7.What can we do more, better or differently to move closer to our objective? Who will do what by when? How will we measure progress?

8.   What concerns do you have?
      (This one can be used anywhere it is needed!)

We would suggest that these are *great* questions, not because we created them, but because the best leaders often use them to achieve the results for which they are noted. Through our leadership research, spanning three decades, we simply discovered the trends.

The best leaders realize that this Framework of questions is not a technique as much as a place to "come from."

Why do the best leaders ask these kinds of questions so often and so consistently? Have they been taught this technique to get people aligned, excited, creative, resolved, focused, etc? For the most part, the answer is a resounding

NO! The best leaders realize that this Framework of questions is not a technique as much as a place to "come from." The precise questions are not as important as the *intention* behind the questions. The Framework for Leadership validates what the best leaders are already doing naturally. Some will even say, "That's what I've already been doing!"

In providing the leadership that transformed the effectiveness of his modern destroyer-class naval vessel to that of attaining the *highest* combat readiness in the history of the Pacific fleet, Commander Mike Abrashoff used the essence of this Framework. Remember, Mike had never heard of Enlightened Leadership Solutions – the company or the book. He just did what worked! He certainly didn't pace around the ship thinking, "Let's see, I should start this meeting with Step 1 of the Framework!" Mike naturally focused on the right things, because that was what he discovered he needed to do to be effective. And so it is with the best leaders.

The Role of Intention

Think about the role of the intention that lies behind the questions you ask, or for that matter, the statements you make. If you're really upset with someone who made a big mistake, asking, "What are you trying to accomplish?" – as innocent as that reads on paper – may come across as very threatening. So, even more important than specific wording is your underlying agenda with the questions, and your timing in using them.

Taking this concept a little further, if you're upset about something, you cannot be emotionally Forward Focused at the same moment. It's impossible. The people around you will sense that you're upset and their fears will come up. When this happens, individual and team effectiveness is compromised. In order to provide effective leadership, you must deal with your own emotions – whatever that takes – before you can get back to a productive intention. Otherwise, you are likely to react and create additional problems.

The Intent of the Framework for Leadership

The intent of the Framework as a whole is to optimize the effectiveness with which a group or team achieves its mission, vision or goal.

Let's look at the intent behind each of the individual steps, or questions:

1. What is already working, or what successes are we having?

The fundamental intent of this step is to coax individuals, groups or teams into being solution-focused (Forward Focused) rather than problem-focused. An additional intent is to build the creative energy of the individual or group in preparation for resolving the issue or meeting the challenge in later steps. To accomplish these "hard" intents, an underlying and primary intent is to have the people involved feel honored for who they are, what they have already done, and open to the possibility of what more they could be and achieve. Without that intent, the question doesn't work. The Step 1 question is a tool for initiating a high-performance environment and it can be very effective, as long as it's backed by the right intention.

> **If everyone who read *Leadership Made Simple* were to make just this one change – to start looking for and analyzing successes consistently – this book would make a significant difference.**

2. What made it work, or caused the success?

The underlying intent here is to learn from past successes so they can be repeated. Now, if the *real* intent is to find out what went wrong, who screwed up and the reason why, you'll never take this Forward Focused question seriously. If everyone who read *Leadership Made Simple* were to make just this one change – to start looking for and analyzing successes consistently – this book would make a significant difference. It's a big opportunity for everyone who wants to provide leadership.

3. What are we trying to accomplish?

The intent of Step 3 is to get everyone on the *same* page and make sure it is the *right* page. This makes sure that everyone is pulling in the same direction, thus maximizing the group's efforts. It's about alignment.

This question also provides an opportunity to continually challenge the status quo – a key responsibility of leadership.[18] How has the situation changed such that our objectives might need to be revisited? Or, what is a higher-level goal that is even more inspiring? Or, are the current objectives still appropriate? These are important reflections. The Step 3 question invites that reflection.

This goal-setting step also defines the gap between where you are and where you want to be, the problem that must be solved or the challenge met – in a Forward Focused manner.

4. What are the benefits of achieving our objectives (for each of the stakeholders)?

The intent here is to determine that everyone is clear and committed to the goal. When people are really clear about "what's in it for them," you don't need to worry so much about getting things done. When people are clear about their personal benefit, buy-in and motivation are high for achieving the objective. It's also an opportunity to make sure the benefits equal or outweigh the efforts needed to achieve the goal.

5. What can we do more, better or differently to move closer to the objective? Who will do what by when? How will we measure progress?

This is where the "rubber meets the road." The entire Framework for Leadership up to this point is designed to prepare for this step – the Action Plan. The intent here is to tap into the creativity unleashed from the positive environment established in the earlier steps.

This step represents a Forward Focused approach to dealing with obstacles, challenges, problems and issues. Remember, the problem is nothing but the gap between what's already working and what we want to accomplish. These Step 5 questions generate the action plan and the accountability that helps close that gap. Step by step implementation of that plan moves us closer and closer to the objective. The plan also establishes how we will measure our success.

The Natural Leader

A person or leader who is "coming from" the true intent of the Framework for Leadership, then, is naturally and continually:

- Looking for successes to celebrate and opportunities to acknowledge people – to let them know they are appreciated and get them Forward Focused.

- Learning from those successes and encouraging others to do the same.

- Assuring that the team or individual is focused on the right objectives and challenging the status quo.

- Making sure everyone is clear about the personal benefits they will receive from being part of the solution, as well as understanding the benefits to all the stakeholders – knowing that both these factors will dramatically impact the outcome.

- a) Developing increasingly better solutions by tapping into the enhanced creativity, enthusiasm and commitment that were developed with the other steps;
  b) assuring accountability for the implementation of the plan;
  c) assuring clarity on how to measure progress.

Again, the very best leaders do this naturally. It is just who they *are*. They are not so much "doing" as "being." It's where they "come from."

The vast majority of us are undergoing individual processes of "becoming" – becoming the best leaders we can be, the best person we can be, the best spouse, the best father or the best mother or friend.

For those of us in this "becoming" phase, the Framework for Leadership is a powerful model and tool for achieving new levels of effectiveness and being. By consciously using the essence of the Framework in what we do – with the right intention behind our actions – we will be encouraged by the results we get. This will stimulate us to keep doing it. The more we use the essence of the process, the better results we will get, and the more it will become part of who we are.

Not only are the results we achieve with the Framework continuously improving and sometimes transformational, but the people around us are transformed as well. When people are immersed in an environment epitomized by the essence of the Framework for Leadership, they are motivated and inspired to be the best they can be. They can and will develop toward that personal ideal, discovering their uniqueness in the process. You'll know this is working when they start running on the questions even before you ask them!

Perhaps the ideal leader reflects part of the essence of the ideal spouse – one who completely and fully accepts the partner for who they are at the moment, while encouraging them to be the absolute most they can be. That is like the leader continually coming from the place of acknowledging someone for their successes, strengths and value – honoring them for who they are right now, while concurrently encouraging them to perform the best they can and become the most they can be. That concurrent focus is a fine balance, and it represents the essence of the Framework for Leadership.

Indeed, not only are the people around you transformed, but the more you practice the essence of the Framework for Leadership, the more you *become* the essence of what it represents. The day you realize that you aren't thinking about Steps 1 through 5, that you are just naturally behaving from the perspectives they represent, you'll know that you've been transformed.

Personal Challenge

We'd like to end this work with a personal challenge.

- **Where could you use the essence of this Framework for Leadership in the next seven days that might make a difference?**

- **How could you use it for an important meeting, a project review, a conflict you must resolve, a performance review, launching a new initiative, or getting a team better aligned and focused?**

Whatever the need, we invite you to experiment with it during the next seven days. If you do that, we believe the Framework for Leadership will be your "friend for life!"

Enjoy the process of personal transformation as you practice the essence of *Leadership Made Simple!*

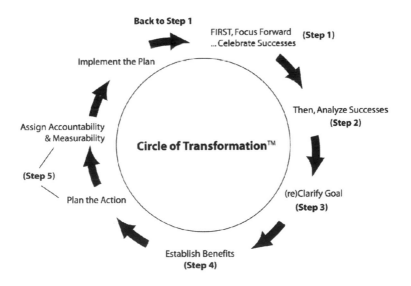

Notes

1. Warren Bennis, "Learning to Lead," *Executive Excellence,* January, 1996.

2. Margaret Wheatley, Ph.D., *Leadership and the New Science,* (San Francisco, CA, Berrett-Koehler Publishers, 2001), p.3.

3. Jack Trout, *The Power of Simplicity: A Management Guide to Cutting Through the Nonsense and Doing Things Right,* (McGraw-Hill, 1999), p. ix.

4. Ronald Heifitz and Donald Laurie, "The Work of Leadership," *Harvard Business Review*, February 2000.

5. Eli Goldratt, *The Goal,* (Croton-on-Hudson, NY, North River Press, 2nd Revised Edition, May, 1992).

6. Wheatley, p. 38.

7. Ed Oakley and Doug Krug, *Enlightened Leadership: Getting to the Heart of Change,* (New York, Simon & Schuster, 1994).

8. As hard as we looked, we could not find specific information about *Vista* magazine. We only have the article torn out with the comments handwritten by Dr. Deming. Our apologies.

9. The authors were first introduced to the power of "asking the right questions" by Kurt Wright, Clear Purpose Management, and author of *Breaking the Rules: Removing the Obstacles to Effortless High*

Performance, while Ed was still at Hewlett- Packard. Doug and Ed wrote extensively on "Effective Questions" in *Enlightened Leadership.*

10. Goldratt.

11. Joel Arthur Barker, "The New Business of Paradigms," video, (Chicago, IL, Advanced Training Source/ATS Media), 2001.

12. Holly J. Morris, "How to Make Yourself Happy," *U.S. News & World Report,* September 3, 2001.

13. William Bridges, *Managing Transitions: Making the Most of Change,* (Reading, MA, Perseus Book Group, May 2003).

14. Noel Tichy with Eli Cohen, *The Leadership Engine: How Winning Companies Build Leaders at Every Level,* (New York, NY, HarperBusiness, 1997), p. 42.

15. Michael Abrashoff, *It's Your Ship: Management Techniques from the Best Damn Ship in the Navy,* (New York, NY, Warner Business Books, May, 2002), p.45.

16. Carol A. Bergmann, *Managing Your Energy at Work: The Key to Unlocking Hidden Potential in the Workplace,* (Bloomington, IN, Authorhouse, 2003).

17. Tichy, p. 8.

18. Tichy, p. 28.

Index

About the Authors

Ed Oakley

After receiving a masters degree in engineering from Stanford University, Ed Oakley spent 15 years in the computer industry, mostly with Hewlett-Packard, managing as many as 300 people. He has been on a continuing quest over the last 30 years to understand how to bring out the very best in people, teams and organizations. He is CEO of Enlightened Leadership Solutions, Inc. (www.enleadership.com), a multi-million dollar consulting and training firm focused on balancing the "hard" and "soft," the processes and people, to create measurable solutions. His engineering orientation insists on practical, simple solutions – an exceptional strength of Enlightened Leadership Solutions.

Ed is a well-known speaker, facilitator and consultant. He holds the National Speaker's Association's Certified Speaking Professional award, and has been well-received by managers from over 65 countries. He specializes in talent selection and development and team dynamics.

Ed has also authored numerous articles, book chapters, audios, videos and learning programs, including Making Managers Into Leaders™.

Doug Krug

Doug is co-author with Ed of the best-selling book, Enlightened *Leadership: Getting to the HEART of Change* (Simon & Schuster). In its 33rd printing, the book is used as a textbook in numerous colleges and universities, as well as corporate and government leadership development and change management programs.

Doug's primary role is helping top executive teams create and sustain the focus and alignment essential to successfully deal with today's most pressing leadership challenges. The essence of Doug's work is built around the premise that the core of what makes a leader cannot be taught – not in the traditional sense. It has to be brought out from within the individual.

With a diverse career as an entrepreneur and management consultant, Doug has proven skills for effectively creating powerful organizational results. Doug provides inspiration and information, giving participants tools that are immediately applicable. Groups actively participate in their own discovery through simple yet powerful exercises.

Enlightened Leadership Solutions, Inc.

Enlightened Leadership Solutions integrates assessment, consulting, training and support products to help you break down your most complex people and process challenges into achievable steps and solutions. We utilize the essence of the Framework for Leadership in all of our work. We know the "answers are in the room."

Our mission is to strengthen your ability to manage change, create a high performance culture and produce sustainable results. We are passionate about helping you produce results that transform your organization and enhance your value to your customers.

Our services focus on balancing two critical areas:

Talent Solutions

Selecting, developing, engaging and retaining the right people who will thrive in your environment, culture and business model.

Organizational Performance

Ensuring your vision is supported by the right structure, roles and processes enabling your people to perform at their best.

ENLIGHTENED
LEADERSHIP
SOLUTIONS

Breakthroughs in Organizational Performance

5380 South Monaco Street, Suite 700
Greenwood Village, CO 80111
303.729.0540
www.enleadership.com
contactus@enleadership,com

Leadership Made Simple Opportunities

We trust you have had a good experience in reading *Leadership Made Simple,* and we want to help you in your successful implementation of the *essence* of the Framework for Leadership™.

To do that we want to announce:

A free periodic journal of practical leadership tips.

This journal will take up where the book leaves off, providing specific, simple and practical tips for being the best leader you can be.

To sign up for the Leadership Made Simple Journal, go to: www.leadershipmadesimple.com.

We look forward to continuing to support you through this free journal. Sign up now before you forget!

Thank you for all the ways you are demonstrating the essence of *Leadership Made Simple*!

Your appreciative authors,

Ed Oakley and Doug Krug